FOCUS

This is a book to which many teachers will say "Hallelujah." It challenges educators and policymakers alike to focus on what's most important and not become distracted by numerous "fads." If we can get our schools focused on the elements Schmoker identifies, more teachers will be achieving dramatic results in their classrooms.

–David T. Conley, director of the
Center for Educational Policy Research, University of Oregon

In his most ambitious book to date, Mike Schmoker moves beyond generalities about education in the United States to offer *very* specific advice on how to improve schools, the curriculum that should be taught in different subject areas, and the way in which curriculum should be taught. Any educator who is willing to consider thoughtful critiques of traditional practices and the thinking behind those practices will be intrigued (and challenged) by Schmoker's ideas.

–Richard DuFour, educator and coauthor of
*Learning by Doing: A Handbook for Professional
Learning Communities at Work*

Mike Schmoker says all we need to know about making school reform work in three words: simplicity, clarity and priority. A sustained focus is indeed what has been missing from almost all educational reforms for the past 30 years. In a book that beautifully practices what it preaches, the author clearly and simply lays out a sensible plan for making school reform focused and coherent. With candor and without political correctness, Schmoker has mapped out a truly effective path for school reform that all educators can grasp and follow.

–Grant Wiggins, president of Authentic Education
and coauthor of *Understanding by Design*

In an age where teachers are forced into the unrealistic pursuit of unobtainable standards, finally, a book emerges that cuts through the noise and helps us return to sensible, authentic teaching. *Focus: Elevating the Essentials to Radically Improve Student Learning* is insightful, practical, and, above all else, inspiring—a must read for all teachers, administrators, board members, and policymakers. Reading this book has made me a better, more reflective teacher.

–Kelly Gallagher, educator and author of
*Readicide: How Schools Are Killing Reading
and What You Can Do About It*

Mike Schmoker gets it right in this trenchant diagnosis of why American schools are failing: Even when the teachers are all good, the school curriculum is a poorly organized clutter that diffuses students' attention rather than focusing it on the essentials they need to learn to be college-ready. Schmoker's book itself is a model of how to cut through the curricular clutter in precisely the way schools need to do.

–Gerald Graff, 2008 president of the Modern Language Association and author of *Clueless in Academe: How Schooling Obscures the Life of the Mind*

This is a brave, powerful book, brimming with good ideas and plain-spoken common sense. Forswearing the fads of the day, Schmoker reminds us of what the sales force of "new and improved" professional development wants us to forget: We already *know* what good teaching looks like—and we've known it for a while. The real question is: Do we have the will to make it happen? This short but powerful book shows us the way.

–Sam Wineburg, Margaret Jacks Professor of Education, Stanford University

Mike Schmoker has provided another valuable resource for all educators. Each one of his books seems to provide more assistance than the previous one. If you admired his earlier writings in the *Results* trilogy you won't be able to put this newest entry down. Once again, he provides a simple way to do a complex thing while at the same time supplying a roadmap for real classroom and school improvement. Just think how we might impact student learning if we all put his ideas to work.

–Greg Netzer, principal of Van Horn High School, Independence, Missouri

Mike Schmoker's new book is brimming with ideas that I immediately want to pass along to the principals, teachers, and district leaders I work with—how we can slim down the curriculum to the essential core; what really effective English, science, social studies, and math lessons look like; how we can get students reading and writing *much* more in class; and how teacher teams can work together with a renewed focus on results. This book is learned, accessible, packed with specific examples, and powerfully convincing.

If you read one book this year, read this one!

–Kim Marshall, educator and author of *Rethinking Teacher Supervision and Evaluation*

Mike Schmoker nails it again. His guidelines for clarifying what we teach and how we teach should bear positive results across this great land. What matters most is what happens in the classroom. Let's focus on making this a nation of readers and the rest will follow.

–Carol Jago, president of the National Council of Teachers of English

FOCUS

ASCD MEMBER BOOK

Many ASCD members received this book as a
member benefit upon its initial release.

Learn more at: **www.ascd.org/memberbooks**

FOCUS

Elevating the Essentials

To Radically Improve Student Learning

MIKE SCHMOKER

Alexandria, Virginia USA

ASCD®

1703 N. Beauregard St. • Alexandria, VA 22311 1714 USA
Phone: 800-933-2723 or 703-578-9600 • Fax: 703-575-5400
Website: www.ascd.org • E-mail: member@ascd.org
Author guidelines: www.ascd.org/write

Gene R. Carter, *Executive Director;* Judy Zimny, *Chief Program Development Officer;* Nancy Modrak, *Publisher;* Scott Willis, *Director, Book Acquisitions & Development;* Carolyn Pool, *Acquisitions Editor;* Julie Houtz, *Director, Book Editing & Production;* Ernesto Yermoli, *Editor;* Greer Wymond, *Senior Graphic Designer;* Mike Kalyan, *Production Manager;* Cynthia Stock, *Typesetter;* Kyle Steichen, *Production Specialist*

Printed in the United States of America. Cover art © 2011 by ASCD. ASCD publications present a variety of viewpoints. The views expressed or implied in this book should not be interpreted as official positions of the Association.

All web links in this book are correct as of the publication date below but may have become inactive or otherwise modified since that time. If you notice a deactivated or changed link, please e-mail books@ascd.org with the words "Link Update" in the subject line. In your message, please specify the web link, the book title, and the page number on which the link appears.

ASCD Member Book, No. FY11-4 (Jan. 2011, PSI+). ASCD Member Books mail to Premium (P), Select (S), and Institutional Plus (I+) members on this schedule: Jan., PSI+; Feb., P; Apr., PSI+; May, P; July, PSI+; Aug., P; Sept., PSI+; Nov., PSI+; Dec., P. Select membership was formerly known as Comprehensive membership.

PAPERBACK ISBN: 978-1-4166-1130-1   ASCD product #110016
Also available as an e-book (see Books in Print for the ISBNs).

Quantity discounts for the paperback edition only: 10–49 copies, 10%; 50+ copies, 15%; for 1,000 or more copies, call 800-933-2723, ext. 5634, or 703-575-5634. For desk copies: member@ascd.org.

Library of Congress Cataloging-in-Publication Data

Schmoker, Michael J.
  Focus : elevating the essentials to radically improve student learning / Mike Schmoker.
    p. cm.
  Includes bibliographical references and index.
  ISBN 978-1-4166-1130-1 (pbk. : alk. paper)
  1. Effective teaching. I. Title.
  LB1025.3.S384 2011
  371.102—dc22

                          2010038950

20 19 18 17 16 15 14 13 12 11   1 2 3 4 5 6 7 8 9 10 11 12

For Ted Sizer, 1932–2009,
who truly understood education reform

FOCUS

Elevating the Essentials
To Radically Improve Student Learning

Introduction

When the number of initiatives increases, while time, resources and emotional energy are constant, then each new initiative . . . will receive fewer minutes, dollars and ounces of emotional energy than its predecessors.

Doug Reeves

* * *

The real path to greatness, it turns out, requires simplicity and diligence. It requires clarity, not instant illumination. It demands each of us to focus on what is vital—and to eliminate all of the extraneous distractions.

Jim Collins

* * *

Hedgehogs see what is essential and ignore the rest.

Jim Collins

The argument of this book is simple: If we choose to take just a few well-known, straightforward actions, in every subject area, we can make swift, dramatic improvements in schools. Some believe we could virtually eliminate the achievement gap within a few years. An Australian study indicated it would take seven years (Garnaut, 2007); another study estimates about five years (Kane & Hanushek in Haycock, 2005).

But the price for such swift improvement is steep: Most schools would have to stop doing almost everything they now do in the name of school improvement. Instead, they would have to focus only on implementing "what is essential." Hardest of all, they would have to "ignore the rest" (Collins, 2001, p. 91)—the fads, programs, and innovations that now prevent us from ensuring that every student in every school receives a quality education.

Why such draconian action? Because the only reason our schools haven't made astonishing progress in the last 30 years of "reform" is quite simple: very few schools ever implemented "what is essential"—the most powerful, simple actions and structures that would dramatically increase the proportion of students prepared for college or careers.

What is "essential" for schools? Three simple things: reasonably coherent curriculum (*what* we teach); sound lessons (*how* we teach); and far more purposeful reading and writing in every discipline, or *authentic literacy* (integral to both what and how we teach). But as numerous studies demonstrate, these three essential elements are only rarely implemented; every credible study confirms that they are still pushed aside by various initiatives, every year, in the majority of schools (Schmoker, 2006).

The status quo has to change. We insult and frustrate our teachers and leaders when we keep asking them to adopt complex, confusing new initiatives and programs that can't possibly succeed in the absence of decent curriculum, lessons, and literacy activities. These constitute the indisputable—if age-old—core of effective practice, and of education itself.

In the last few years, I have found that educators yearn to be told something like this:

There will be no more initiatives—at least for a time. Instead, we will focus *only* on what will have an immediate and dramatic impact on learning in your classrooms: ensuring the implementation of a common, content-rich curriculum; good lessons; and plenty of meaningful literacy activities (such as close reading, writing, and discussion) across the curriculum. Moreover, we will not expect you to implement these elements until we have fully clarified that these three elements will—indisputably—have more impact on your students' success than all other initiatives combined.

If we understand and embrace the concept of simplicity, which starts with a recognition that "less is more," then our schools will achieve what previous generations never thought possible. Best of all, none of the essential elements must be implemented perfectly to have their intended effect. Throughout this book, I'll be citing ordinary schools and teachers who implement the elements in ordinary, imperfect ways and still achieve spectacular results.

About This Book

In Section 1, we'll examine the power of simplicity applied to *what* and *how* we teach. Chapter 1 describes how simplicity is a benevolent but jealous taskmaster, allowing us to focus on only a few carefully selected priorities at a time. Indeed, any initiative we adopt *before the three essential elements are implemented* only postpones their implementation and their impact on student learning. Without these three elements in place, any initiative is doomed; it is built on sand. This is the primary lesson of the last 30 years of reform.

Chapter 2 clarifies the simple, essential elements of *what* we should teach, including *literacy*—reading, writing, and talking. These elements would ensure that virtually all students would be prepared for college, careers, and citizenship. Such an education is not new, but it is at the center of the most enlightened conceptions of "21st century" learning (which must be distinguished from its more faddish, commercially driven counterparts). Moreover, if we want all practitioners to have "piercing clarity" (Collins, 2005, p. 17) about what to teach, we need to take a hard-headed look at standards—both state and national. We need to be smart, even wary, consumers of these documents. Intended to simplify and clarify course expectations, they often complicate and confound our attempts to provide a coherent, quality curriculum in every course. (And curriculum is perhaps the single largest factor that affects learning—see Marzano, 2003). Chapter 2 ends with a discussion of standards documents followed by a brief, simple guide to selecting essential standards for any course.

In Chapter 3, I clarify and simplify *how* we should teach to dramatically and immediately enhance any teacher's impact on student learning. How we teach is also inseparable from literacy. We'll examine the simple, age-old fundamentals of *good lessons:* their pedigree and new research on the stunning and immediate impact such lessons would have if most teachers began to actually implement them consistently. Chapter 3 ends with two straightforward templates that incorporate these fundamental elements. Variations on these two simple templates could be used for all or most of our teaching, in every subject area. We've complicated teachers' lives for long enough. It is time to simplify their work in ways that make them *more* effective, with *less* effort and frustration.

Chapters 4 through 7 make up Section 2. In these chapters, I describe both *what* and *how* we can effectively teach in each of four subject areas (the only ones I feel equipped to address at this time): language arts, social studies, science, and math. We'll learn how to navigate the challenges of standards documents in each subject; language arts and math are particularly in need of clarity and simplification. For each of the disciplines, I'll share how experts advocate for the same core practices—especially authentic literacy, or the intensive integration of purposeful reading, writing, and talking into each subject.

In addition, throughout Section 2, I give extended treatment to the need for large helpings of current news and opinion pieces in class. I will make a prediction here. If we take this seriously, it will have a game-changing impact on everything we hold dear: student engagement and retention, college preparation for all, and attitudes toward school—by students and teachers.

Finally, in every chapter, I repeat the main elements and arguments of this book. This is by design. In writing and rewriting these chapters, I felt the necessity to stay very close to the three essential elements of *how* we teach, *what* we teach, and *authentic literacy* while adding, in the right measure, layers of clarity and specificity. I hope this repetition helps to clarify our work as well as the need to embrace such priority-driven repetition in school improvement efforts.

Once again, the argument of this book is that to break the grip of 30 years of feckless, failed reforms, we must focus on three matters first—*and these alone*—until they are at least reasonably well implemented in any school. If we do this, the impact will be swift and it will be breathtaking.

Let's begin by looking at the concepts that makes these wonderful aspirations possible: *simplicity, clarity,* and *priority.*

SECTION I

First Things First: *What* We Teach,
How We Teach—and Literacy

1

The Importance of Simplicity, Clarity, and Priority

s odd as it sounds, simple, well-known strategies and structures drive improvement in any organization (Pfeffer & Sutton, 2000). In education, this means that the general underperformance of schools can be directly attributed to a failure to implement three simple, well-known elements: a common curriculum, sound lessons, and authentic literacy. We love to talk about these elements. But we have never fully clarified them or obsessed over their implementation. And we haven't done enough to clarify the astonishing impact these three elements would have if they were even reasonably well implemented.

As Allan Odden writes, our failure to improve schools in the last few decades isn't because we lack funding or don't know how to improve schools. What we lack is the "will and persistence" to implement *what we already know* (Odden, 2009, p. 22). Or as Collins writes, the key to success is not innovation; it is "simplicity and diligence" applied with fierce devotion to our highest priorities (Collins, 2001b, p. 104).

First Things First

Let's begin with a general description of what should be our highest priorities, which we will continue to clarify in Chapters 2 and 3 (and for the subject areas in Chapters 4 to 7). I will often use terms like "decent," "sound," and "reasonably good" when referring to these elements. This is to stress that they are so potent they do not need to be implemented perfectly or with any special skill. Their profound impact will come largely from *all teachers applying them consistently and reasonably well*. Then, as teachers continue to work in teams to practice and refine their implementation, even better results will ensue. We can count on this.

Here are the three elements that we should approach with "simplicity and diligence," until they are satisfactorily understood and implemented in every subject area.

1: What We Teach. This simply means a decent, coherent curriculum, with topics and standards collectively selected by a team of teachers from the school or district—that is *actually taught*. The number of "power standards" (Ainsworth, 2003a) must not be excessive; it should account for about half of what is contained in our standards documents (Marzano, 2003). This allows us to teach the essential standards in sufficient intellectual depth, with adequate time for deep reading, writing, and talking. Why is this so important? Because such "guaranteed and viable curriculum" (Marzano, 2003, p. 22) is perhaps the most significant school factor that affects learning. But such a curriculum is found in very few schools (Berliner, 1984; Marzano, 2003; Schmidt, 2008).

2: How We Teach. Think of this simply as ordinary, structurally sound lessons that employ the same basic formula that educators have known for decades but few implement consistently. As we'll see in Chapter 3, this formula was formalized some 50 years ago (but is, in essence, thousands of years old). Yet the impact of such lessons, if we implemented them with even rough consistency, would be jaw-dropping (Wiliam, 2007). We'll look at the evidence for this in Chapter 3. Importantly, the pivotal feature of effective lessons is the conscientious effort, throughout the lesson, to ensure that all students are learning each segment of the lesson before moving to the next one.

3: Authentic Literacy. Authentic literacy is integral to both what and how we teach. It is the "spine" that "holds everything together" in all subject areas (Phillips & Wong, 2010, p. 41). In this book, "literacy" or "authentic literacy" simply means purposeful—and usually argumentative—reading, writing, and talking (Lunsford & Ruszkiewicz, 2009). (As we'll also see, explanations and summaries are forms of argument.) Literacy is still the unrivalled, but grossly under-implemented, key to learning both content *and* thinking skills. But authentic literacy is categorically different from the so-called "reading skills" and pseudo-standards that have wrought such havoc in language arts. We'll be looking at the case for very different kinds of literacy standards in Chapter 4.

It is worth emphasizing here that implementation of the above elements will benefit immeasurably when teachers work in teams—that is, in true "professional learning communities" where curriculum and lessons are continuously developed, tested, and refined on the basis of assessment results (DuFour, DuFour, Eaker, & Many, 2006; Schmoker, 2006).

Believe this or don't: These three elements, if even reasonably well-executed, would have more impact than all other initiatives combined. In the great majority of our schools, they will do more than any other combination of efforts to ensure that record numbers of students learn and are prepared for college, careers, and citizenship. A content-rich curriculum, sound lessons, and authentic literacy would wholly redefine what public schools can accomplish with children of every socioeconomic stratum. Because of this, their satisfactory implementation should be our most urgent, jealously guarded priority—the ongoing focus of every team meeting, every professional development session, every faculty and central office meeting, every monitoring and reporting effort. *Until these elements are reasonably well implemented,* it makes little sense to adopt or learn new programs, technology, or any other innovations. To be fair, any innovation is fair game once these elements are implemented if—but only if—that innovation does not in any way dilute or distract us from these always-vulnerable priorities.

Does this sound too "simplistic"? Can such simplicity really be the elusive key to better schools? To get some perspective, let's step outside our own profession for a moment.

The Power of Simplicity, Clarity, and Priority

Consider a football team that loses about half of its games, year after year. (There is some autobiography here; I coached football for a short time.) Each week, the coaches scour the Internet to find new, complex plays and offensive schemes. This confuses the players, who never mastered the last set of plays. All the while, the coaches never fully note something very boring but important: the performance of their offensive line. If they paid attention to what every coach knows, they would notice that their offensive linemen have never sufficiently mastered the fundamentals of effective blocking, like footwork and body position. If even reasonably well executed, these fundamentals make a tremendous—literally, "game-changing"—difference. And so the solution to this team's mediocre performance is really very simple: The coaches need to stop confusing the team with new plays and start focusing strenuously on the most mundane, but hugely effective, blocking techniques until they are implemented success-fully. The palpable results—measured in successful plays, first downs, points scored, and games won—would be immediate and dramatic.

Now imagine a hospital where infection rates are high. (This is a true story.) At this hospital, all doctors know the five basic procedures that inhibit infection. These procedures, according to one doctor, "are no-brainers; they have been known and taught for years." But alas, doctors don't consistently implement them, even as they continue to attend various trainings in complex, cutting-edge practices and procedures. *In fact, the doctors (like the football coaches) aren't fully cognizant that these simple, well-known procedures are directly linked to results (i.e., mortality infection rates).* The solution to this hospital's problem is simple, not complex: A checklist is generated, and its importance is made crystal clear to doctors. In addition, the faithful use of the checklist is monitored to ensure that all doctors implement it properly and consistently. The result? Infections immediately plummet from 11 percent to 0 percent! In two years, these stunningly simple procedures prevent eight deaths and save the hospital approximately $2 million in lawsuits. All this without any complex, high-tech, or cutting-edge solution (Henig, 2009).

If we educators can't see ourselves and our schools in these two examples, I fear for us. They are both analogous to our failure in schools, where the simple elements of common curriculum, effective lessons, and the most ordinary but authentic kinds of literacy practices are well known but almost never clarified, reinforced, or monitored. As a result, they are rarely implemented (Schmoker, 2006). And that, friends, is the simple reason we haven't made enormous strides toward better schooling in this age of reform.

Our failure to be clear and focused prevails even as we continue, year after year, to attend conferences, workshops, and book studies; adopt complex programs and initiatives; divide students into groups based on their respective "learning styles"; and "integrate technology" into our instruction—all while denying students a coherent curriculum, sound lessons, and meaningful opportunities to read and write.

As a matter of record,

• The actual curriculum an average child learns, in the same course and in the same school, varies tremendously from teacher to teacher; what you learn depends on what teacher you have.

• Despite the central importance of reading and writing to general learning and college preparation, students rarely engage in authentic reading and writing activities, even in language arts.

• Teachers routinely call on students *who raise their hands* throughout the course of most lessons (vivid confirmation that teachers aren't clear on the most critical elements of a good lesson).

Studies confirm that these conditions prevail in the overwhelming majority of our classrooms (Pianta, Belsky, Houts, & Morrison, 2007; Allington, Lezotte, Berliner, Rosenholtz, and others in Schmoker, 2006).

Clearly, the simple elements of effective schooling outlined here should be our highest priorities—implemented first, before we adopt any other initiative. Perhaps we should require a warning label like this one on all notices of upcoming workshops, trainings, conferences, or book studies:

> **WARNING:** If you or your staff do not already implement a reasonably sound, common curriculum that covers an adequate amount of subject-area content; that is taught with the use of the most essential, well-known elements of effective lessons; and that includes ample amounts of meaningful reading and writing, *then please don't sign up for this.* This training will have no effect on learning in your classroom or school. Master the fundamentals first. Then, if you still need this workshop (and you might not), we look forward to seeing you. Have a nice day.

Three Books That Reinforce the Power of Simplicity

Priority is a function of simplicity, and it dictates that we only focus on a few things at a time—namely, on those elements that are most likely to help us achieve our goals. Our priorities are plainly out of whack. The following three books can help us further understand the importance of simplicity, clarity, and priority.

Good to Great, by Jim Collins

Jim Collins reveres simplicity; he uses the word countless times in his book *Good to Great* (2001a). Collins found that "the essence of profound insight" into organizational improvement "is simplicity" (2001a, p. 91). That's why, as many know, he reveres hedgehogs, which do one thing well (roll into a ball to protect themselves), as opposed to foxes, which plan and plot and scheme as they "pursue many ends at the same time." Foxes aren't simple; they are "scattered and diffused, moving on many levels" (p. 91). That's why they fail. By contrast, hedgehogs, with their simple, singular focus, succeed because they commit entirely and exclusively to "what is essential and ignore the rest" (Collins, 2001a, p. 91).

On some level, schools know "what is essential." But we don't clarify or reinforce our priorities as often or as passionately as we should. It is very hard for us to "ignore the rest," the endless bombardment of new programs or innovations that look so good but distract us from those few, powerful actions and structures that are the soul of good schooling.

There is an iron law at work here: We will never master or implement what is most important for kids if we continue to pursue multiple new initiatives *before* we implement our highest-priority strategies and structures. Collins had schools in mind when he wrote that effective social-sector organizations suffer from an addiction to doing many things instead of just a few. To succeed, he notes, we must "attain piercing clarity about how to produce the best long-term results, and then exercise the relentless discipline to say, 'No thank you' to opportunities that fail the hedgehog test" (2005, p. 17).

The Knowing-Doing Gap, by Jeffrey Pfeffer and Robert Sutton

Simplicity, clarity, and priority are intimately linked. For an organization to maintain a focus on its highest priorities, it must simplify and repeatedly clarify them so that everyone in the organization knows implicitly what to do and *what not to do*.

But priorities are fragile and high-maintenance. Without frequent, repeated clarification, we start to drift from them. The priorities inevitably start to mean different things to different people. If priorities aren't incessantly simplified and clarified, they are always at the mercy of the next new thing, our natural forgetfulness, and a failure to protect the best (often *old, already-known*) practices from the encroachment of new, but less effective, practices or programs.

Jeffrey Pfeffer and Robert Sutton are the authors of *The Knowing-Doing Gap.* According to them, leaders resist simplicity; they are often irrationally enamored with novelty and complexity, which prevents them from focusing on and implementing their core priorities (2000, p. 33). The result is stagnation or decline. "Complexity," the authors warn, "interferes with turning knowledge into action" (p. 55). Unfortunately, many leaders have a natural prejudice against "old ideas and simple prescriptions"—even though, if implemented, these old, simple ideas are the key to better results (p. 53). Many leaders would rather launch new initiatives, regardless of their effectiveness. Why? Because it distracts them from the harder work of seeing to it that their highest, simplest priorities are implemented— "actually done" (p. 54).

In contrast, successful organizations aren't enamored with novelty, technology, or complexity; they know that "success depends largely on *implementing what is already known*" (p. 14, my emphasis). They know that "simple prescriptions" conveyed with "clarity and simplicity" are the hallmarks of effective action and leadership (p. 55). At the successful companies profiled in Pfeffer and Sutton's book, "implementation of simple knowledge" was the main driver of improvement (p. 15).

It is critical that schools learn the lesson that "best practice" in effective organizations is rarely *new* practice. On the contrary, the most effective actions are "well-known practices, with the extra dimension that they [are] *reinforced and carried out reliably*" (p. 14).

The implementation of coherent curriculum; effective lessons; and abundant amounts of purposeful reading, writing, and talking should be our highest priorities. Are they currently "reinforced and carried out reliably" in most schools? Not even close, according to every credible study going back to the 1970s (Schmoker, 2006). We would rather innovate than follow up to ensure that our priorities are implemented.

To ensure that our best practices and structures are truly and efficiently implemented, we must make constant, unwavering efforts to *clarify, reinforce, and reward* their implementation by teams and teachers. This brings us to the fascinating findings of Marcus Buckingham.

The One Thing You Need to Know, by Marcus Buckingham

Marcus Buckingham's work is the perfect complement to *The Knowing-Doing Gap*. Buckingham reinforces the importance of simplicity—the principle that we accomplish more when we focus on less. In *The One Thing You Need to Know*, he reports that organizations must carefully determine their highest priorities, their focus—even if it is only "one thing." Having done so, organizations should then expend enormous amounts of organizational energy clarifying and simplifying those priorities—and resist any pursuit that could detract from them.

After analyzing survey data, Buckingham found that employees crave simplicity and clarity; they want to know precisely what they can do to be most effective—and then not be distracted from that. Their highest priorities—the "core"—must be clarified incessantly. "Clarity," writes Buckingham, "is the antidote to anxiety . . . if you do nothing else as a leader, be clear" (2005, p. 146). Commenting on his interviews with employees in multiple organizations, he writes that "everywhere, the wish was the same: 'Get me to the core'" (p. 3). That is, relentlessly clarify and communicate to us what actions will make us most effective. Then, don't throw new initiatives at us that divert us from the core. Protect us, as Becky DuFour writes in her excellent review of Buckingham's book, from new initiatives that wash upon school employees "in waves" (2007, p. 69).

To protect the core, leaders must work diligently to "filter" what comes into the organization—the ceaseless assault of new programs and trainings that seduce employees away from the core—in our case, from actually monitoring and implementing sound curriculum, effective instruction, and authentic literacy. Effective organizations "sift through the clutter" (Buckingham, 2005, p. 188) and don't allow it to divert employees from their highest priorities. They "apply disproportionate pressure in a few selected areas." This "lopsided focus" fuels people's productivity, creativity, and morale (p. 26). Less is more.

Leaders must be seen as clarifiers, focusers, "keepers of the core" who incessantly "cut through the clutter . . . to distinguish between what is merely important and what is *imperative . . . those few things you must never forget*" (p. 26, my emphasis). But to ensure the implementation of our priorities, we must monitor that implementation. As Buckingham writes, "The old truisms tell us that 'what gets measured gets managed' and 'you get what you inspect' and they survive as truisms because they are manifestly true" (p. 176).

It's this simple: If we want better schools, we have to monitor the implementation of our highest priorities. Schoolchildren will continue to wait until we monitor and ensure that our priorities are being implemented.

Let's now look at how these simple truisms play out in some of the organizations Buckingham describes.

Carefully Protected Focus at Best Buy. Research revealed that the success of Best Buy's sales force hinged on one simple thing— the ability of salespeople to master and then confidently explain the different features of the products they sold. That's it. That is their number-one, carefully protected focus. Since making this discovery, they have said "no, thank you" to anything that might interfere with this priority. In an industry where new products are constantly flooding the market, Best Buy made a bold decision: They reduced their product line by 50 percent so that salespeople could fully master their core inventory. Best Buy knows that to preserve the core, it must discard an existing product every time it adds a new one. This is the secret to the company's soaring success (p. 155).

Apple Computer and One Thing. Similarly, Apple Computer has been invited to embark on numerous new initiatives and partnerships. But Steve Jobs has strenuously resisted heavy lobbying from those within and outside of the company and stayed true to one thing: "figuring out how to invent cool technology but making it wonderfully easy to use." Jobs is as proud, he said, "of the things we have not done as I am of the ones we have done" (p. 165).

Borax: Safety at the Core. To get an even closer glimpse of the practical actions that allow companies to stay true to their priorities, let's look at Buckingham's description of how Borax ensured that its core practices were, in Pfeffer and Sutton's (2000) words, incessantly "reinforced and carried out reliably" (p. 14). The Borax mine is north of Edwards Air Force Base in California. The company's in-house research revealed that its simple core was safety: If it could keep its employees safe from on-the-job accidents, then morale, efficiency, and profitability would take care of themselves. And they did—on every metric (Buckingham, 2005, pp. 167–174).

Borax knew that the key to protecting the core focus was communication. Leaders constantly reminded, trained, and told stories to make sure that people understood the outsize importance of safety procedures. At Borax, every meeting began with an anecdote about how injuries were averted by employees. Safety procedures and effective practices were clarified and demonstrated. Leaders displayed and celebrated measurable benchmarks, like the number of days without an accident, and progress toward monthly and annual accident-reduction goals. All of these actions helped employees see that their efforts to stay safe afforded them both financial security and good health. And profits soared commensurately.

Like the other companies in Buckingham's book, Borax succeeded because they reinforced their priority through constant clarification and communication, including what Buckingham regards as the single most powerful way to motivate productive action: recognition and celebration.

Simplicity, Clarity, and Priority in Education

In schools, leaders should collect and share analogous data on how many classrooms consistently exhibit common curriculum, sound lessons, and authentic literacy. We should celebrate gains in any of these areas as we guide and advise teachers at faculty meetings. And we should celebrate gains made each grading period on common assessments that themselves reflect the level of implementation of these three areas. (For detailed procedures and rationale for such leadership practices, see *Results Now*, Chapters 9 and 10 [Schmoker, 2006]).

What can we expect when a single teacher or a whole school focuses only on its simplest priorities—its core? The following two brief cases should allow anyone to see the possibilities.

Simplicity, Clarity, and Priority in the Classroom

Some might remember a teacher I described in my book *Results Now* (Schmoker, 2006). His teaching consisted of the oldest, best-known curriculum and teaching practices, and was rich in authentic literacy practices. His only technology tool was an overhead projector. I observed him a few times during his first year at the lowest-achieving high school in our community. Watching him, I had an epiphany: All he did was *actually teach* a sound English curriculum, rich in reading and writing, using ordinary, structurally sound lessons (those which incorporate the same basic elements we've known for half a century). I will elaborate on these in later chapters, but in essence, he taught whole-class lessons focused on a clear learning objective in short instructional "chunks" or segments, punctuated by multiple cycles of guided practice and formative assessment ("checks for understanding"). And he did this every day. He was neither particularly charismatic nor theatrical. He was what any teacher or team can be, if liberated from the new programs and initiatives we force on teachers every year. Interestingly, *none of his teaching in any way reflected any recent innovations or programs whatsoever.*

The result? The success rate in his classes alone was so high that his *entire school* made the largest writing gains of any high school in the state (from 59 percent to 85 percent passing the high school exit exam). More startling still, his school outperformed the other two schools in the city, despite their overwhelming demographic advantages. His simple, effective teaching and curriculum obliterated the socioeconomic factor.

Simplicity, Clarity, and Priority in One School and One District

Years ago, I was fortunate enough to teach at a middle school where both curriculum and instructional priorities were made crystal clear. They were clarified in the interview process and reinforced at every faculty and department meeting. For those of us teaching English, priorities included the expectation that students would regularly write and revise two to three substantive papers per grading period. Moreover, priorities were reinforced and clarified at every faculty and department meeting. All professional development was internal, organized by department heads. No popular fads or programs or innovations were pursued or implemented.

Instructional leadership in the building was simple, and it strictly reinforced our priorities. Every faculty and department meeting reinforced the elements of effective teaching we had all learned. The principal monitored the implementation of the curriculum and the elements of effective instruction by conducting one or two brief classroom walkthroughs each month. She also met briefly with teachers quarterly to discuss end-of-quarter evidence of student performance (e.g., grade book data, the number of books read and papers written). If the data from these conferences or observations revealed a concern, the teachers would be asked to observe and meet with others in the school who taught the common curriculum effectively; the teachers were then expected to teach in the same fashion. If they preferred not to, they would not be back the following year.

As a result of this stunningly simple model of leadership, every teacher in that school *actually taught* the curriculum and *actually provided* sound lessons, almost every day, in line with what we all know about effective instruction. Of course, some did these things better than others—but all did them. There was no test prep whatsoever, but test scores at this school were among the very highest in the state. Of even more importance, I would estimate that *all students* in that school read and wrote four to five times as much as students in typical schools. Every student was truly being prepared for college.

Simpler still: In the district where this school was situated, teacher advancement was based on demonstrated proficiency in all of the above. There were no annual initiatives or "strategic plans" to get in the way of our simple core: a year-to-year insistence on sound curriculum, sound instruction, and authentic literacy. The district made this model crystal clear to principals—and reinforced it accordingly.

That is simple, powerful leadership, and essentially similar to what we know about Adlai Stevenson High School in Lincolnshire, Illinois, known for its stunning success with professional learning communities. Even so, the similarities are striking. Stevenson began its celebrated journey with a focus on only two things:

1. Directing teams of teachers to create and help each other to implement a quality, common curriculum for every course (the first foundational step toward improvement).

2. Directing the teams to ensure sound, ever-improving instruction and lessons. To ensure implementation, leaders (including teacher leaders and department heads) met with teams each quarter to discuss progress on common quarterly assessments (which had to have a hefty writing component).

Stevenson stayed focused on these things *for five years*, resisting any temptation to add or adopt new programs. All professional development during this period was internal—most of it occurring in the team meetings (which are the best form of staff development). In addition, leaders at Stevenson routinely recognized and celebrated measurable success and progress on common assessments at every meeting.

That is leadership.

• • •

A simple, emphatic insistence on common curriculum, sound lessons, and authentic literacy ought to be our common goal—the standard for our profession at the classroom, school, and district level.

Schools need to focus exclusively on these same, simple priorities for years—or until virtually every student can be assured of reasonably good curriculum and instruction in every course, every year, regardless of which teacher they are assigned.

For this to happen, we need to be sure that *what we want* from our schools is precisely *what we communicate*—simply, clearly, and persistently.

If, in this new century, we wish to prepare unprecedented numbers of students for college and careers, regardless of demographic factors, the ball is in our court: We simply need to be as obsessive about our "core" as Best Buy and Borax and the schools discussed in this chapter are about theirs. We need, as Jim Collins tells us, to define our priorities with "piercing clarity" and then say "no, thank you" to anything that would divert us from successfully implementing them.

In the next two chapters, I will clarify the fairly simple—and mostly traditional—conceptions of what I believe should be our highest priorities: the reasonably effective implementation of good curriculum, effective instruction, and authentic literacy. I hope that, once I describe what the conceptions are and the profound and immediate impact they will have, you will agree that it is foolish to pursue any other initiatives until these are satisfactorily implemented.

What We Teach

21st century skills . . . are not new, just newly important.

Elena Silva

• • •

21st century learning is not new but represents what our best educators have been teaching us for several centuries.

Jay Mathews

• • •

What's new today is the degree to which economic competitiveness and educational equity mean these skills can no longer be the province of the few. . . . State, national, and international assessments show that despite a two-decade-long focus on standards, American schools still are not delivering a content-rich curriculum for all students.

Andrew Rotherham, founder, 21st Century Schools Project

What we teach—a guaranteed and viable curriculum—matters immensely. Curriculum may be the single largest factor that determines how many students in a school will learn (Marzano, 2003). Because of the curriculum's outsize impact, my aim in this chapter (and Chapters 4–7, on the subject areas) is to simplify and clarify its most essential features. In clarifying good curriculum, I will cite the work of some of the most enlightened advocates of 21st century education. Please don't confuse them with some of their more high-profile, commercially driven counterparts, whose "inchoate" notions of education have been rightly ravaged (Maranto, Ritter, & Levine, 2010, p. 25).

The advocates of 21st century education cited in this chapter are not urging us to rashly reinvent curriculum around technology or group projects (though there is room for both—once we have implemented our highest priorities). They are not proposing (as some do) that students need to spend less time learning content and more time making movie previews, video skits, wikis, silent movies, or clay animation figures. We need to say "no, thank you" to such faddish, time-gobbling activities.

The people I'll refer to are urging us to go back to the future, to embrace—at long last—a powerful combination of the following strategies for *all* students:

- Adequate amounts of essential subject-area content, concepts, and topics;
- Intellectual/thinking skills (e.g., argument, problem solving, reconciling opposing views, drawing one's own conclusions); and
- Authentic literacy—purposeful reading, writing, and discussion as the primary modes of learning both content and thinking skills.

As the epigraphs at the top of this chapter suggest, none of this is "new"; none of it is unique to this century. What *is* new is the recognition that now, more than ever, all students need—and deserve—such an education. The demands of 21st century careers and citizenship are increasingly similar to what students need to be prepared for college—whether they decide to attend college or not. It is increasingly clear that the primary reason so many students don't even have the option of attending college is our manifest failure to provide a coherent, content-rich curriculum that includes adequate opportunities for them to read, write, and talk thoughtfully (Allington, 2001; Conley, 2005; Hirsch, 2009; Rotherham, 2008; Schmoker, 2006). We have to eradicate the hidden curriculum that covertly, if unintentionally, deprives so many students of such an education, without their consent.

Preparation for College, Careers, and Citizenship—for All

For too long, we have indulged in errant, offensive notions about who is or isn't "college material." Yet the demands of college, careers, *and* citizenship are increasingly the same and can be met by almost any student who learns from a reasonably decent, literacy-rich curriculum. One study, by ACT, found about a 90 percent overlap between the needs of workers and those who attend college, and recommends that "all high school students should experience a common academic core that prepares them for both college and workforce training, *regardless of their future plans*." Another study, by The American Diploma Project, came to the same conclusion: that the needs of the workplace are "increasingly indistinguishable" from the knowledge and skills needed for college success. The U.S. Chamber of Commerce calls these studies "right on target" (Olson, 2008, p. 19).

As we will see, there is absolutely no reason that a decent K–12 education cannot provide virtually all students with what they need to be active, informed citizens, effective workers, and—if they choose—college students. We need not resolve the thornier question of whether all students should go to college. Simply: if we did our job in schools from the start, such an education would be attainable by all—or tantalizingly close to all—students.

Needed: A Moment of Candor

Common sense should tell us that any semblance of a decent curriculum should and could contain a "common academic core"—generous amounts of good content and critical thinking skills, and sufficient opportunities to learn to read, write, speak, and listen effectively. Anything less than this is only a pretense of "curriculum"—a sham. Yet such sham curriculum, according to most studies, is quite common in our schools, even in the "honors" track (Schmoker, 2006).

The problem is not that we lack resources. As Allan Odden writes, "The problem isn't funding." It is the lack of "will and persistence" to implement *what we already know* (Odden, 2009, p. 22). Nor do we lack time; we have 12 years with our students and almost 1,000 instructional hours per year. That's enough to educate almost anyone, but not if we continue to squander these hours, every day, on nonacademic activities. The problem is that the actual taught curriculum is marked by a stark, irrational absence of the most fundamental knowledge and literacy skills needed to do well in college or university.

Let's be frank: We all know college grads who aren't particularly brilliant, disciplined, or intellectually oriented. We know, with a moment's reflection, that the requirements for earning some kind of degree from any number of two- and four-year institutions are hardly prohibitive or unrealistic. So if we sincerely desire to make college an option for record numbers of students, our task is simple: We need to reclaim the hundreds of hours each year that are now spent on nonacademic tasks. We need to redirect those hours toward the most simple, obvious tasks that prepare students for college, careers, and citizenship: *meaningful reading, writing, speaking, and thinking—around an adequately coherent body of content in the subject areas.*

In this regard, the 21st century could be the moment we come to our senses and finally implement a simple, substantive curriculum—and then sit back in amazement at its impact on students from every social stratum.

Let's now listen to some prominent advocates of 21st century education.

Content-Rich Curriculum and Literacy for All

As Phil Schlechty, author of *Schools for the 21st Century* (1990), notes, "Too many children leave school without having developed the skills, attitudes and habits of mind that will equip them for life in the 21st century" (1997, p. 2). The civic, intellectual, and workplace demands of the new century, writes Schlechty, will require that *all students* can "read, write and cipher . . . think and solve problems . . . draw upon a rich vocabulary based on a deep understanding of language and the human condition" (1990, p. 40).

This is hardly what students now get, even in our better schools (Pianta et al., 2007; Schmoker, 2006; Wagner, 2008). Note Schlechty's emphasis on literacy, problem-solving, and deep knowledge of "language and the human condition." These form the basis for authentic literary studies, the social sciences, history, and geography (or "global studies"). But as Schlechty avers, we can't be satisfied with only providing such an education to the most privileged (1997, p. 12). We need to provide such an "elite education for *nearly everybody*" (1997, p. 40, my emphasis).

Our current system, alas, doesn't even attempt to provide this kind of rich, rounded education for all. Reflecting on this, Schlechty observes, "There is a crisis and it is real" (1997, p. xv). Interestingly, he says this in response to David Berliner and Bruce Biddle's widely read 1995 book, *The Manufactured Crisis,* which also contains an incisive call to 21st century education.

Skills for the 21st Century

Many have cited Berliner and Biddle's book to defend the status quo. They misread the book. *The Manufactured Crisis* contains a bracing critique of typical schooling, of both *what* and *how* we teach. The authors emphatically call for a curriculum rich in content, advanced literacy, and thinking skills. And they lament their manifest absence.

In a section titled "Skills for the 21st Century," the authors report that we have never provided an intellectually demanding, content-rich curriculum to most students. Their observations are as penetrating now as they were in 1995. Even then, they could see us lurching toward technology in the hope that it would save education, even before we attended to the much higher priorities of curriculum and instruction.

Despite years of lip service, schools have never made the "cultivation of thoughtfulness" a priority. Like John Goodlad (1984) before them, Berliner and Biddle found that students are seldom asked to read and resolve "conflicting views," to exercise judgment, or to engage in "critical thinking" (pp. 298–299). In the 21st century, schools must ensure that all students become "citizens who are flexible, who embrace new ideas, who can reason well when faced with complex new ideas" (p. 300). All students need abundant opportunities to speak, write, and listen—"to make and evaluate . . . logical arguments[,] . . . solve problems, [and] offer potential solutions to problems" (pp. 300–301). And all benefit from opportunities to connect literature to their lives, to "create meaning from related readings," and to do their own research (p. 319).

Berliner and Biddle's understanding of 21st century curriculum includes a ringing endorsement of a shared body of subject-area content. "Let there be no mistake," they write; students need to learn and acquire a common "knowledge base that constitutes our cultural heritage . . . our country badly needs a citizenry that shares such a heritage" (p. 302).

Content matters. And educators need to be very clear on the relationship between content and our ability to think and reason.

Content *and* Intellectual Skills: More of Both

Any credible curriculum has to embody the link between knowledge and critical thinking (usually done as we read, talk, or write).

Andrew Rotherham, former head of the Progressive Policy Institute's 21st Century Schools Project, laments our failure to provide a content-rich curriculum to students (Rotherham, 2008). This has serious ramifications, he notes, as

> content undergirds critical thinking, analysis, and broader information literacy skills. To critically analyze various documents requires engagement with content and a framework within which to place the information. It's impossible, for instance, to critically analyze the American Revolution without understanding the facts and context surrounding that event. (2008, p. 1)

E. D. Hirsch (2008) similarly argues that the abilities to argue, evaluate, and reason are "attained by studying a rich curriculum in math, literature, science, history, geography, music and art and *learning higher-level skills in context* . . . there is a scientific consensus that academic skill is highly dependent on specific relevant knowledge." Acquiring such knowledge is the result of a "slow, tenacious and effective buildup of knowledge and vocabulary" (p. 40). Happily, this critical buildup is best acquired through disarmingly simple, age-old teaching methods that can be captured in two simple, versatile templates (described in the next chapter).

Both Rotherham and Hirsch have an important ally in Daniel Willingham, the prominent cognitive scientist. In "Education for the 21st Century: Balancing Content Knowledge with Skills," he too criticizes the disparagement of content knowledge by some well-known 21st century organizations. Critical thinking is in fact highly dependent on content knowledge. We can't understand, much less critically evaluate, the ideas in a textbook, newspaper, or magazine *if they contain too much unfamiliar information.* If we don't know enough about the subject we're reading about, we may bog down and become confused as we read (2008).

Pursuing Knowledge and Thinking Skills Together

As we'll see in subsequent chapters, and as Willingham makes clear, we have always learned content best through thinking skills and activities, starting—and this is refreshing—in the earliest years:

> The ability to analyze and to think critically requires extensive factual knowledge . . . facts must be taught, ideally in the context of skills and ideally *beginning in preschool and even before.* (Willingham, 2009b, p. 19, my emphasis)

We acquire knowledge and thinking skills best when we learn them reciprocally, when we are asked to read, write, argue, and problem solve as we engage with text and with an organized body of essential knowledge. As Elena Silva notes, "there is no reason to separate the acquisition of learning core content . . . from more advanced analytical and thinking skills [and again], *even in the earliest grades"* (2008, my emphasis).

Willingham found that we learn and retain information best when we have a chance to evaluate or think about it. He suggests we give students *"simple tasks"* that allow them to intellectually engage with the content they are learning (2009a, p. 63). We'll be looking at lots of such "simple tasks" built around questions and prompts in subsequent chapters.

Thoughtful engagement with content knowledge should include a redoubled emphasis on textbooks as well as sources of current information, like newspapers and magazines. I will demonstrate how we can make routine use of these in all subject areas. Let's now look very closely at what advocates of 21st century education have to say about advanced levels of literacy, long assumed to be the province of the college-bound. Advanced literacy can be acquired by all, using simple, endlessly repeatable activities.

Literacy as the "Spine"

• • •

Think of literacy as a spine; it holds everything together. The branches of learning connect to it, meaning that all core content teachers have a responsibility to teach literacy.

Vicki Phillips and Carina Wong,
The Bill and Melinda Gates Foundation

• • •

As we've seen, there is a clear convergence of thought about the importance of a "common academic core" that prepares students not only for college but also for careers and citizenship. That academic core includes a liberal component of authentic literacy skills. The importance of high levels of college-oriented levels of reading, writing, and speaking cannot be overemphasized in K–12 education.

Priority: All-Pervasive Literacy

How important is literacy? Let's listen again to E. D. Hirsch (his "verbal competence" is a close synonym for literacy):

To impart adequate verbal competence is the *most important single goal of schooling* in any nation. Verbal scores are reliable indexes to general competence, life chances and civic participation. Good verbal scores diminish the notorious income gap. Decades of data show that the earnings gap between racial and ethnic groups in the United States largely disappear when language competence in Standard English is factored in. (2010, p. 31)

Or consider the words of Vince Ferrandino and Gerald Tirozzi, the former and current presidents, respectively, of the National Association of Elementary School Principals and the National Association of Secondary School Principals. I cite them in every presentation I deliver:

> Under-developed literacy skills are the number one reason why
> students are retained, assigned to special education, given long-
> term remedial services and why they fail to graduate from high
> school. (2004, p. 29)

It is impossible to overstate the importance of literacy. Yet nothing so begs for clarity—and simplification—in K–12 education. In
my last book, *Results Now!* (2006), I wrote at some length about
authentic literacy and the startling state of literacy education in our
schools. Because literacy is so important, so foundational to learning
in every subject, we must be crystal clear about *what it is* and *what
it is not.* Let's listen to some people whose work helps us to achieve
clarity about literacy in its simplest and most liberating forms.

"Plain Old Reading and Writing" in the 21st Century

"The most valued people in the 21st century," writes Howard
Gardner (2009), are those who "can survey a wide range of sources,
decide which is most important and worth paying attention to, and
then put this information together in ways that make sense to one-
self and, ultimately, to others . . . [they] will rise to the top of the
pack" (p. 18). Thomas Friedman, author of the bestseller *The World
Is Flat: A Brief History of the 21st Century* (2005), concludes that the
most successful people in this century will be those who can acquire
and use knowledge to develop and communicate creative combinations of ideas, applications, and strategies to solve problems.

How are these 21st century abilities acquired? From something
he sees as in alarming decline: "plain old reading and writing" (p.
353). Friedman cites Marc Tucker, the author of the 1986 report *A
Nation Prepared: Teachers for the 21st Century.* Tucker's organization,
the Carnegie Task Force on Teaching as a Profession, recommends
a broad liberal arts curriculum that includes "a very high level of
preparation in reading, writing, and speaking" (Friedman, 2005, p.
319). But as Friedman observes, these skills have taken an enormous

hit. Fewer students than ever can read the kinds of "lengthy, complex texts" required to learn and innovate (pp. 353–354). The reason for this is simple: Our schools simply don't require students to read texts of increasing length and complexity, starting with textbooks. This pattern begins in the earliest grades, and it persists right up through graduation (Duke, 2010; Gomez & Gomez, 2007).

Textbooks? Yes!

Though it may sound hopelessly unfashionable, textbooks (as we'll see in later chapters) are a greatly underestimated resource for learning essential content and acquiring literacy skills. In "Reading for Learning: Literacy Supports for 21st Century Learning" (2007), Louis and Kimberly Gomez write that the new century will routinely require students to "critically analyze and synthesize information" gleaned from the kind of dense, complex prose found in textbooks. They are so important that our current failure to make them a prominent part of schooling may be the primary reason for "poor student performance in the content areas" (p. 225). Gomez and Gomez recommend that "broad-based efforts to make text more prominent should be redoubled" (p. 228).

In an incisive *Educational Leadership* article, Kathleen Cushman describes the "culture shock" most students are in for when they arrive at college. Having rarely read and never been taught to read textbooks, they lack the "deeper reading, writing and inquiry that college requires" (2007, p. 47). This is one of the main reasons they drop out in such large numbers.

But how should students approach textbooks—or the literature, poems, or op-ed pieces we should be providing for them in abundance? With questions. Nothing could be simpler. Teams in every subject area must make the creation and refinement of such questions among their highest priorities.

Questions and Texts: An Essential Combination. There is nothing complicated here. Much of a good education consists, as it always has, of a simple combination of one or more good texts matched with an interesting question. We simply teach students to read deeply and purposefully to answer such questions—and to then discuss and write (even briefly) about the text and what they learned from it. This is the essence of both learning and literacy. As Peter Cookson writes, "Socrates believed that we learn best by asking essential questions and testing tentative answers against reason and fact in a continual . . . circle of honest debate" (2009, p. 8).

It is especially important for teams of teachers in every discipline to make the development and refinement of good, text-based questions among their highest priorities. My best teachers and professors came to class with carefully prepared questions for whole works or for individual sections or chapters. These were the heart of our inquiry as we read and discussed and wrote our way toward an education. Teams of teachers can do this even more effectively and thus share the load of developing interesting lines of inquiry for the various texts they teach in a course.

Such inquiry-driven learning, reading, and discussing should periodically culminate in more extended writing and, for certain assignments, public presentations—which have become, as Arnold Packer points out, "essential in the 21st century job market" (2007, p. 2).

Papers and Presentations. One place that emphasizes reading, discussing, writing, and presenting is the New York Performance Standards Consortium, which has received awards for being a model of 21st century education (see their website at www.performance assessment.org). In this network of 28 schools, the focus is on literacy—on close reading, discussion, and writing in every course. All students write lengthy, complex, end-of-course essays and graduation projects in each discipline, based on wide reading and research. These are all judged with common rubrics. For continuous improvement purposes, data are gathered yearly to determine areas of strengths and weaknesses per the common performance rubrics. In addition, all seniors must deliver a presentation based on one of their papers to a panel of judges from the school and community. Students write papers with titles like "Why Do They Have to Die? An Analysis of the Protagonists' Deaths in *Dr. Jekyll and Mr. Hyde, Metamorphosis*, and *Of Mice and Men.*"

As the consortium's director, Ann Cook, told me, students who left other schools thrive in the consortium schools and do better in college than their counterparts. And—significantly—*teachers love working in the consortium*; the schools involved seldom have openings (Schmoker, 2008–2009).

In some places, we're beginning to formalize such deep, authentic literacy. It's great to see how the state of Rhode Island has started to require a senior research paper and presentation for high school graduation (Schmoker, 2008–2009). In my conversations with Rhode Island administrators, I have found that they are very encouraged by the benefits this requirement is already having for students.

We have to hope such literacy-driven requirements are the wave of the future. I think we should require a research paper and a public presentation from students at the end of 5th, 8th, and 12th grades. *Their performance on these or on end-of-course papers should be among the primary data we use for purposes of accountability and continuous improvement.*

Literacy is integral to both what and how we teach; it's the spine that holds everything together and ties content together in every subject. The best teaching emerges from this simple combination of a good question and good text—in every subject. If such work seems daunting or complicated, fear not: As we'll be seeing in the next chapter, literacy is best taught using (and reusing) variations on the same age-old template, year after year, in every course.

Less Is More: Conley's "Standards for Success"

I have already discussed some of my favorite 21st century thinkers. But perhaps my very favorite is David Conley, so frequently cited in articles about 21st century education. For me, the work done by Conley and his colleagues represents a stunning opportunity for us to achieve true simplicity and clarity about literacy and to make a bold—but necessary—move away from the least worthy subject-area standards (the worst of which, as we'll be seeing, are found in English language arts). Conley and his colleagues conducted a landmark, in-depth study of the skills and content students need to succeed in college. The study's findings are based on a review of hundreds of college syllabuses and interviews with hundreds of students and professors, and can be found in Conley's *College Knowledge* (2005). I'm especially attracted to that book's short, simple list of the primary intellectual skills we should impart to K–12 students. These "standards for success," or (as they are alternately referred to) "habits of mind," operate as both thinking and literacy skills for all disciplines.

Conley and his colleagues found that the following four intellectual standards were paramount, within and among the disciplines:

1. Read to infer/interpret/draw conclusions.
2. Support arguments with evidence.
3. Resolve conflicting views encountered in source documents.
4. Solve complex problems with no obvious answer.

These four simple habits of mind can powerfully inform student reading, writing, and talking in every discipline. For that reason, I will be referring to them (or their approximations) throughout this book and in the subject area chapters. But even more radically, I believe these four standards could productively replace *almost all* of our current K–12 English language arts standards, as well as the confusing verbiage that accompanies standards in areas like science and social studies. Matched with disciplinary content, I believe they give us all we need to ensure that students are prepared for college, careers, and any state or national test that comes their way. In fact, I'm sure of it.

Some might prefer to adjust the language of the four standards or blend them with something like Bloom's taxonomy. Fine. But something close to this short, powerful list could be a worthy and effective guide to studies in any discipline. If such standards were the basis for learning good content, for studying various texts, and for building interesting questions, they would *greatly clarify our work at every grade level* and promote success on any state or national assessment, regardless of which way the winds of standards and assessment might blow. This is sure to occur if we take Conley's advice about how much reading and writing students should do to prepare for life after high school.

My recommendations for applying Conley's ideas are mine, not his. But I think his excellent work could help us to greatly simplify our work and to avoid the excesses of national standards.

A New Kind of Standard

Our standards have never described what may be the most vital factor in education: clear, minimal guidelines for how much meaningful reading and writing students should do in every subject area. In addition to the four standards listed above, Conley adds this one: that K–12 education should prepare students to effectively produce multiple three- to five-page papers of the kind they will be regularly asked to write in college—but which are dismayingly rare in high school. The requirement for such writing is so rare that Conley's research team came to this conclusion: "If we could institute *only one change* to make students more college ready, it should be to increase the *amount and quality of writing* students are expected to produce" (2007, p. 27).

And how could this be achieved? With simple, clear parameters for each subject, including the following:

• The precise amount of text and the number of books, including titles to be taught in common by all teachers for a given course;

- The number and length of papers assigned; and
- Common rubrics/criteria by which students will be graded (Conley, 2005, pp. 82–83).

These, in my view, are truer, more legitimate "essential standards" than the majority of the nonsense that now populates our state and national standards documents for language arts. If we upheld such standards, we could discard most of the arcane, confusing ones already in place.

Of course, to be meaningful, the implementation of these standards must be monitored quarterly, with teacher teams sitting down to review common assessment results. This is one of the key but overlooked elements of effective leadership. (Such monitoring and leadership issues are treated in more detail in Schmoker, 2006, Chapter 9.)

I hope I've helped to clarify the general nature of *what* a good education consists of: adequate amounts of content as well as fairly traditional intellectual and literacy skills. We'll see how these play out in the subject areas in Chapters 4–7. But before we move to the next chapter on *how* we teach, let's take a moment to consider the issue of standards themselves at a time when national standards have arrived in earnest. Then we'll review some simple procedures for how we can work from these very imperfect standards documents to select the best, most essential standards for any course or subject area.

A Brief Guide to Selecting Essential Standards

Developing a guaranteed and viable curriculum for every course begins with a real challenge—the perplexing nature of standards documents themselves. This section will clarify, in simple steps, how to select and organize curricular topics and skills into coherent curriculum for any course.

Others have written very helpful and more detailed guides to such work (Ainsworth, 2003a; DuFour et al., 2006; Reeves, 2003). My aim here is to briefly summarize this process, but first I would like to share some personal perspective. I want to encourage a reexamination of standards themselves, without abandoning them. Some may find this material provocative, but my intention is to merely make the selection and use of standards simpler and more fruitful.

The Challenges of Standards Documents

Standards documents can be helpful starting points for building curriculum (though much less so in English language arts, as I will argue). But they are also sources of both confusion and overload. The new national standards for math and English language arts don't necessarily solve this problem; in some ways, they perpetuate it. Bright minds are now questioning the legitimacy of standards themselves, at least as they are currently conceived (Kohn, 2010; Ravitch, 2010). Will these new standards, once they are finalized, truly promote better teaching and learning? If the work done so far in math and language arts is any indication, I am still skeptical. And though the national standards for language arts are better than the state standards they would replace, there are still too many of them, and many are poorly and confusingly written. One prominent expert on standards observes that many of them are merely "pretentious gibberish" (Sandra Stotsky in Garner, 2010, p. 8). I have to agree. Worse yet, dozens of them are dangerously prone to prompting the kinds of test prep and worksheet exercises they were intended to prevent.

It will take years for these issues to be settled. The well-intentioned advocates for the standards are realizing this. Also, *no one really knows how to put the new standards into practice.* There are real fears that poor curriculum materials (advertising "Aligned with national standards!") will flood the market and be purchased indiscriminately by schools and teachers desperate to comply. In a recent meeting of key leaders and sponsors of the new standards, disturbing concerns emerged. As one observer at this meeting noted, when it comes to how to actually implement these standards, there are still "more things still left in the air than resolved" (Gewertz, 2010, p. 19). And we have yet to take on the potentially pricklier subjects of social studies and science.

As I'll be showing, the new language arts standards are almost as troublesome and overwrought as the state standards that preceded them. Shouldn't the new standards and assessments be truly field-tested before they are *required*—of everyone, almost immediately? Shouldn't we, as Diane Ravitch (2010) implores us, study their effects and unintended consequences in pilot schools before we go national? We saw what happened when we let political considerations trump good sense with state standards and assessments: curricular chaos, test prep, and the corruption of language arts.

So what do we do in the meantime, while we wait for standards to be developed for the content areas and for the above issues to be resolved (which will take years, with many setbacks)? Simply: We must make discriminating use of these highly imperfect documents—state or national—to develop good grade-by-grade standards. Once that is done, we can immediately begin to provide an excellent education for all students, one that will prepare them for college, careers, and any test that comes their way. The process is not complicated, but it must begin with a healthy skepticism toward standards—especially their peculiar verbiage.

Topics, Not Verbiage

I have read many sets of standards, state and national, for various subject areas. Many of them have received high ratings from prestigious agencies. I am always bewildered by these ratings, which fail to acknowledge what bloated, confusing, poorly written documents the standards are. Some read like they were never proofread. And we know they were never field-tested at even a single school.

Everyone knows these documents are too large and contain far more standards than can be conscientiously taught. But we should also wonder at the verbs that accompany the topics. Words like "analyze," "identify," "understand," "evaluate," "discuss," and "explain" seem to have been assigned, with other confusing verbiage, almost arbitrarily to their various topics. (I can just hear committee members saying, "We've got too many 'identifies' here. Can we throw in a few more 'analyzes' or 'discusses'"?) And again, what follows these verbs is often incomprehensible; I would have no idea how to teach them.

Keep in mind, too, that many of the standards are mere bluffs. As Furhman, Resnick, and Shepard point out, actual state tests consist of "a grab bag of items only loosely matched to state standards" (2009, p. 28). There is a very tenuous connection between these high-sounding standards and the multiple-choice items on the assessments.

So ignore most of the verbiage surrounding the topics, as E. D. Hirsch (2009) and others recommend. Look primarily at the content topics. Then, once your team has determined which topics you agree on, establish your own higher-order purposes for teaching them.

I would replace the verbiage with something akin to the four intellectual standards described by Conley (read to infer/interpret/draw conclusions; support arguments with evidence; resolve conflicting views and source documents; solve complex problems with no obvious answer). These standards are useful, focused, and aligned with precisely what students need to succeed in college and careers (Conley, 2005).

Now we're ready for the next simple step, which requires confident, bold action.

The Case for Drastically Reducing Content Standards

We should reduce the content contained in most standards documents by about 50 percent—even more in language arts. It stands to reason that if we have fewer standards but teach them *in adequate depth*, students will learn more, retain more, and learn to think. And test scores will take care of themselves.

How much risk is involved in taking this bold but essential step? Not much. Larry Ainsworth and Doug Reeves have worked with schools and districts for many years, helping them to reduce the amount of standards they teach. They start with Marzano's recommendation that we should eliminate *about two-thirds of the standards* (Marzano & Kendall, 1998). According to Ainsworth, he and his colleagues from Doug Reeves's Leadership and Learning Center have had consistent success selecting only a fraction of the standards and making them their priority. Such radical efforts, according to Ainsworth, have "proven themselves again and again over the years *to absolutely work*" (e-mail communication; my emphasis).

We've known for decades that the highest-achieving countries teach fewer than half of the standards we teach to (Schmidt, 2008). Singapore, Japan, and China teach to about a third as many math and science standards—about 15 per grade level compared to our 50 (Leinwand & Ginsburg, 2007).

Oregon recently reduced the number of its math standards by more than two-thirds, allowing teachers to teach in more depth and to connect math to the real world. Educators there have already seen significant growth; at the middle school level, there have been math gains for "every racial, ethnic, and income group" as a result (Hammond, 2009, p. 1). The change has allowed teachers to slow their teaching down and conduct checks for understanding until all students learn concepts. The typical 8th grader in Oregon now performs at nearly the same level as most sophomores.

In Los Angeles, a Title I school adopted Singapore's in-depth approach to math, with its "greatly reduced number of standards . . . a fraction of a conventional American text." The very first year of implementation, the school's students' scores on the California math exam rose from 45 to 76 percent—a 32 percent increase (Landsberg, 2008a).

As Reeves and Ainsworth tell us, making these severe reductions feels risky. But the risk is far greater when we don't make them. This is especially true in the peculiar case of English language arts. I include this discussion here because these standards are foundational to all disciplines, and because the new national standards require them to be integrated into the content areas (a refreshing development, for which the standards developers deserve much credit).

The Special Case of Language Arts

In language arts, "less is more" takes on added meaning. As we'll see in Chapter 4, we may want to abandon or replace the great majority of these standards—or to reconceive them entirely. I'm reminded of two schools that confirm that we can almost ignore conventional language arts standards *and still perform exceedingly well on any test*—while truly preparing students for college.

Tempe Preparatory Academy is a charter school in the Phoenix, Arizona, area. Its achievements attest to what happens when the English curriculum consists almost entirely of the kinds of standards suggested here: close, analytic reading of common texts; monthly formal writing assignments; and daily Socratic discussions where students argue, resolve conflicting viewpoints, and draw their own conclusions. The result? The year high-stakes testing arrived in Arizona, even the highest-achieving schools had enormous failure rates in all three categories—reading, writing, and math. Not so Tempe Prep: In every category, 100 percent of their students passed (the only school in the state to achieve this). We'll hear more about them in later chapters.

View Park Preparatory High School is in South Los Angeles. The language arts curriculum at View Park consists almost exclusively of having students read documents closely and then write argumentative papers using the Toulmin argumentative method. A typical reading and writing assignment would be built around a question like this: "In *One Flew Over the Cuckoo's Nest*, does McMurphy liberate or further imprison his fellow inmates?" (Hernandez, Kaplan, & Schwartz, 2006, p. 51).

What were the results of this minimalist curriculum that virtually ignored the state's language arts standards? View Park, whose student body is 97 percent black, became the highest-achieving high-minority school in the state of California (Hernandez et al., 2006). Ninety percent of the 2008 graduates have been accepted into four-year colleges, many to prestigious universities (Landsberg, 2008b).

Clearly, we need to simplify curriculum—to drastically reduce the number of standards to those with the highest priority. A focus on high-priority standards not only optimizes essential learning, it also ensures good test scores on any state or national assessment. As Doug Reeves (2004) contends, with great logic and clarity, a good set of priority standards addresses about 88 percent of the items on the state test, but not 100 percent. If you go after that extra 12 percent, you will have to cover too many standards and have less time for the truly essential ones. But a focus on the most essential standards promotes both learning *and* higher test scores.

So how do we actually go about reducing standards? That's simple, too.

How to Select Essential Standards

The following is not meant to replace the good work in the best books on selecting the most essential standards. It is only meant to demonstrate how common sense and collective judgment—at any school—can ensure success in selecting what standards we will teach.

First, in all but the special case of language arts, eliminate all or most of the verbs while paying greater attention to nouns and topics. Strip the verbiage from topics like ancient Greece, photosynthesis, the location of the oceans, alternative forms of energy, or Harriet Tubman.

Then, decide on a reduction target (for example, to reduce the number of standards from 60 to 30—or 20). I'm looking at a set of 7th grade history standards as I write this. No one could meaningfully teach more than half of them. We must review the standards and reduce their number. You may want to use criteria like the following, developed by Doug Reeves:

> • **Endurance.** Will the standard provide students with knowledge and skills beyond a single test date?
> • **Leverage.** Will the standard provide knowledge and skills that are of value in multiple disciplines?
> • **Readiness for the Next Level.** Will the standard provide the students with essential knowledge and skills that are necessary for their success in the next grade level? (Ainsworth, 2003b, p. 13)

To make a preliminary determination,

• Have everyone quietly review and select their favorite 40–50 percent of the standards—or even fewer in language arts. (Time limits are helpful here—take about 10 to 15 minutes for the review.)
• Do quick, simple dot-voting or counting to determine which half of the standards get the highest number of individual votes.
• Display the results—the standards with the most votes—on a board or projector.

There is normally a sense of relief here as people immediately see the attraction of such a simplified list. Minus the "clutter" of the less-essential standards, it reveals the opportunity for in-depth instruction of a potent core of agreed-upon topics.

Of course, this list is only preliminary. The team should now discuss the initial draft of "power standards" (Ainsworth, 2003a) and discuss or advocate for the addition of some and the deletion of others. Consider a rule that for any topic added or restored, you remove another to make room for it. Try very hard not to exceed your target (e.g., 50 percent of the standards).

As a penultimate step, lay the standards out on a four-part grid, by grading period, and estimate how many days or class periods to devote to each. This might provoke some additional shuffling and adjustments—and perhaps some more additions or deletions. You might also want to tentatively assign variations on Conley's four intellectual standards/habits of mind to these topics (read to infer/interpret/draw conclusions; support arguments with evidence; resolve conflicting views and source documents; solve complex problems with no obvious answer).

Finally, if some are anxious about this process being too con-straining, I like the recommendation of DuFour and colleagues (2006): Arrange for the common standards not to consume more than 15 or 16 weeks out of an 18-week semester; that leaves some room for teachers to teach their own preferred topics or units.

Ideally, these sets of standards would be reviewed and discussed vertically at some point—to make final adjustments that reduce unnecessary redundancy, build on previous grade learning, and pre-pare students for essential learning at the next grade level. But even grade-level work of this kind (for starters) will profoundly increase coherence and produce equally profound results, because it taps into the powerful factor of "guaranteed and viable curriculum," which is the single largest factor that affects learning outcomes in a school (Marzano, 2003).

Course-alike teams can now begin to develop lessons and units, assign appropriate texts and textbook pages with good questions and prompts, and develop common assessments, starting with end-of-unit and end-of-grading-period assessments. Throughout, they should ensure that lessons and assessments include ample amounts of reading, discussion, and writing.

Importantly: Data from these end-of-quarter and unit assessments become the primary tools for monitoring implementation and promoting improvement. They become the basis for the essential team discussions with the principal, department head, or teacher leaders at quarterly meetings—at the very heart of effective leadership in the professional learning community. As DuFour points out, these meetings are the best means at the leader's disposal to ensure that the essential curriculum is actually being taught (in Schmoker, 2006).

• • •

That's enough general information on *what* we teach; we'll look at additional details in four subject areas in Chapters 4 through 7. Now let's look at the other factor that, coupled with good curriculum, is equally deserving of our exclusive attention in the coming years: *how* we teach.

How We Teach

Improved classroom instruction is the prime factor to improve student achievement gains.

Allan Odden and Marc Wallace

• • •

There is a lot of sitting and listening and not a lot of thinking.

Robert Pianta (on his observations of more than 1,000 classrooms)

• • •

Good teaching is good teaching and teachers don't need to adjust their teaching to individual students' learning styles.

Daniel Willingham

• • •

All available evidence suggests that classroom practice has changed little in the past 100 years.

James Stigler and James Hiebert

W e've been looking at *what* we should teach—at content and skills, including authentic literacy skills. In this two-part chapter, I will clarify *how* we should teach, again including authentic literacy practices. We'll see how nothing, other than *what* we teach, is more deserving of priority.

The most respected educational researchers speak almost as one on this issue. Linda Darling Hammond argues that the single most important determinant of success for students is the knowledge and skills of that child's teacher" (Goldberg, 2001, p. 689). Allan Odden and Marc Wallace observe that "improved classroom instruction is the prime factor to improve student achievement gains" (2003, p. 64). Richard Colvin and Judy Johnson have come to believe that parents and the public deserve far more detailed knowledge of what actually goes on in classrooms. Why? Because of mounting evidence that the teacher's actions can no longer be seen as just one among many factors; teachers are "the most important school factor in how much children learn" (Colvin & Johnson, 2007, p. 36). It is now a well-established fact that even three years of fairly ordinary but effective teaching can completely change the academic trajectory of low-achieving students—vaulting them from the lowest to the highest quartile (Bracey, 2004; Sanders & Horn, 1994).

These facts have finally caught the attention of the popular press. In her recent article in *The Atlantic*, journalist Amanda Ripley describes her encounter with the influence of effective teaching. While reporting on the success of the most effective teachers in Teach for America, she discovered that even in the worst schools, the most simple, ordinary teaching strategies overcome all other factors by significant margins. This is, she writes, "the most stunning finding to come out of education research in the past decade" (Ripley, 2010, p. 2).

What makes these findings most interesting is that "effective teaching" is not some complex combination of talent, technique, or long experience. As Elmore (2000) observes, we are too quick to assume that good teaching is a "mysterious process that varies with each teacher" (p. 16).

As we'll see, anyone can immediately implement the most essential, common elements of good teaching with success—and then get better at them with *practice* (as I and so many other teachers have). Effective instruction consists primarily of just a few ordinary, largely whole-class teaching practices that we have known about for decades. But we have never made the consistent implementation of these practices a priority. As we'll see, the impact of these practices is so profound that Marzano has concluded they should be "routine components of every lesson" (2007, p. 180). Surely this should be among our very highest priorities.

If good teaching can have this much impact, then we had better be perfectly clear about what it is. *Moreover, we cannot afford to overcomplicate the elements of effective teaching.* That will only confuse practitioners and impede the consistent use of these elements. To that end, I will attempt to simplify them. Then, in the second part of this chapter, I will describe two enormously effective (and utterly unoriginal) teaching templates. In combination, these overlapping templates could be used by any teacher, new or veteran, to deliver 80 percent or more of the curriculum in any course or grade level. These elements simplify teaching while ensuring that students learn content knowledge and thinking and literacy skills with unprecedented pleasure and efficiency.

Effective Lessons: A Refresher Course

• • •

Sometimes the first duty of intelligent men is the restatement of the obvious.

George Orwell

• • •

[We must resist] the default mechanism that directs us to study and learn more rather than to take action using what we already know.

Peter Block

• • •

Despite their limitless differences, effective lessons share the same, well-known core structure. Though terms may differ, the essential parts of a good lesson include a clear learning objective with some effort to provide background knowledge or create interest in the topic, teaching and modeling, guided practice, checks for understanding/formative assessment, and independent practice/assessment (which can be one in the same).

There's nothing new here. These terms were formalized almost half a century ago, but their essence is as old as teaching itself. Let's now look at them in more detail.

Clear Learning Objectives. The learning objective should be a topic, skill, or concept selected from the agreed-upon curriculum. Some examples:

- Solve first-degree polynomial problems.
- Write an effective introductory paragraph for an argument.
- Make inferences/draw conclusions about a character (literary or historical).
- Compare and contrast meiosis and mitosis.

These are very different from the pseudo-objectives taught in many lessons: Complete these problems, fill out this worksheet, read and answer the questions, watch a movie, or make a poster/mobile/PowerPoint presentation about [fill in the blank]. Good objectives are clear, are legitimate, and derive from a decent, agreed-upon curriculum. But how do we teach them?

Teaching/Modeling/Demonstrating. As we'll see, these are often variations on lecture or direct teaching—explaining, demonstrating, instructing. But mere teacher talk doesn't assure learning. Two more elements are critical, and often simultaneous: guided practice and checks for understanding (a near-synonym for the most common forms of "formative assessment").

Guided Practice. Throughout the lesson, at brief intervals, the teacher must allow students to practice or apply what has been taught or modeled while he or she observes and guides their work. This step should include frequent opportunities for students to work in pairs and occasionally in groups, as they are often the best teachers *and translators* of what we just (so brilliantly and eloquently) taught. This step overlaps with the next, as our ability to "guide" student practice is only as strong as our ongoing attempts to find out if or how well students have learned.

Checks for Understanding/Formative Assessment. Though I use both terms almost synonymously, I prefer "checks for understanding" because it is the older term, referring to the simplest forms of formative assessment. I believe our formative assessment efforts need to begin with the simplest forms of checking for understanding. This step is especially critical to the success of the lesson, yet is still seldom implemented with consistency. As students practice, and between each step in the lesson, the teacher should conduct "formative assessment" by checking—assessing—to see how many students have mastered that particular step. This ongoing "check for understanding" allows the teacher to see what needs to be clarified or explained in a different way, when to slow down, or when it's all right to speed up the pace of the lesson.

As we'll be seeing, even the oldest forms of checking for understanding significantly increase the proportion of students who learn (as it did for me at a critical stage in my teaching). Here are some simple, common forms of checking for understanding:

- Circulating, observing, and listening as students work in pairs
- Calling on a sampling of students or pairs *randomly* between each step (*not* on students who raise their hands)
- Having students signal their understanding: thumbs up or down; red, green, or yellow Popsicle sticks
- Having students hold up dry-erase boards with answers/solutions

There is nothing new here. What *is* new is the realization that these seemingly "boring and pedestrian" (Collins, 2001a, p. 142) practices are not only effective, but astonishingly so. If they were consistently implemented, we would take a quantum leap toward the goal of "learning for all."

What happens when they are *not* implemented?

The Consequences of Typical, Poorly Built Lessons

Here are two true stories that represent what I see in most schools.

The first focuses on a highly respected teacher in a high-scoring school. He is always innovating. He has initiated interdisciplinary teaching, heavy use of technology, hands-on activities, and lots of "project-based learning." His students do very little reading and even less writing. But they spend lots of time going to and from the library, often preparing, making, and then listening (listlessly) to each other's flashy but unfocused PowerPoint presentations. And like the majority of the teachers at his school, he doesn't even realize that his lessons and projects are devoid of modeling, guided practice, or checks for understanding. Nonetheless, the teacher is highly regarded for his emphasis on "active" learning, on "integrating technology" into his "project-based" assignments. Why? *Because instead of coherent curriculum and effective lessons, these are the school's operative priorities; they are the focus of praise and professional development in his school and district.*

Many miles away, in one of the largest urban districts in the United States, several elementary schools are proud of their gains on standardized reading tests (which garnered good publicity). This is the result of massive expenditure and exceedingly tight supervision to ensure faithful implementation of a scripted reading program. All this work requires an army of additional personnel working from multicolored "data walls" to incessantly test, track, assign, and shuffle students to tutorials and small-group remediation in state reading skills and standards, tested with multiple-choice items just like those on the state test.

But something goes wholly unnoticed: When you visit multiple classrooms, *not a single lesson* is conducted appropriately. A dead giveaway is that whenever the teacher asks a question, he or she then *calls on those students who raise their hands* while the majority of students sit quietly or look around the room. The fundamental elements of teaching, modeling, guided practice, and checking for understanding are never reinforced. Instead, staff members are entirely focused on implementing the intricacies of the complex, scripted program. Further inquiry reveals the logical results of such teaching (despite their marginal gains): About 80 percent of students fail on daily assignments, creating the need for expensive, time-gobbling remediation mechanisms. Worst of all, no one notices that the focus on multiple-choice drill in language arts standards means that there is *never time for students to read or write for an extended time, or to read an entire book*. All students read are the dull, low-quality materials provided by the scripted basal reading program. Awash in publicity, it never dawns on the program coordinators that if teachers taught even reasonably sound lessons, they could get far better results at little or no extra expense. This would allow students to spend more time in meaningful reading and writing activities, which would actually prepare them for college.

I cannot exaggerate how common such practices are. I see these basic narratives played out everywhere I go. Educators continue to be diverted toward new methods and programs, even as the most important aspects of curriculum, teaching, and literacy are ignored almost entirely.

To change these circumstances, both the elements of and the case for sound lessons need to be articulated clearly, emphatically—and repeatedly. Let's now look carefully at the convergence of research on the powerful elements of good teaching. Then we'll look at the exciting, unprecedented impact we could be having if we made these elements and coherent curriculum our highest priority.

Research on the Elements of Effective Lessons

Each of the following researchers has done detailed work on the elements of a good lesson. My purpose here is simply to show how research points to a clear, indisputable convergence on the primacy and power of these simple elements of good instruction—the ones that would have the most immediate and significant impact *if they were implemented* in most classrooms.

Madeline Hunter

We have to begin with Madeline Hunter, who worked in the 1960s and 1970s. Divorced (as they often are) from good curriculum, her recommendations could devolve into a dull formula. But today we realize that her basic model is the key to ensuring that all students learn the most worthy content and intellectual skills. More than anyone, Hunter helped formalize the basic moves of an effective lesson, and she coined many useful terms that are still with us.

Hunter advocated that lessons begin with crystal clarity about what students are to learn from a given lesson. Once clarified, the lesson should always begin with an "anticipatory set"—some attempt to create interest or curiosity in the topic by providing background or by asking a provocative question. This is to be followed by direct teaching and modeling in small, manageable steps.

Between each (brief!) step, the effective teacher implements two hugely effective techniques reciprocally: guided practice and checking for understanding. This cycle must occur *multiple times during the lesson* until the greatest number of students has learned the material (Marzano, 2007; Popham, 2008). These whole-class teaching methods are effective almost immediately, even in classrooms with a range of levels and abilities. Any teacher who adopts them can expect to multiply the number of students who learn *within days of adopting them.*

Let's now look at some prominent researchers who have expanded on Hunter's work.

Douglas Fisher and Nancy Frey

Doug Fisher and Nancy Frey have built on Hunter's simple lesson structure in their recent book *Checking for Understanding* (2007). In their work, they advocate for lessons based on the "gradual release of responsibility" model. That is, students are given increasing amounts of responsibility to work on or complete an assignment independently on the basis of multiple iterations of "guided instruction" (their term) alternating with—and informed by—checks for understanding throughout the lesson.

Like Hunter, Fisher and Frey emphasize that students must have plenty of opportunity to work in pairs (and occasionally in groups), which is one of the most effective ways to promote understanding for all—and keep boredom at bay.

Importantly, an effective lesson pivots on our use of formative assessment—of checking for understanding. As Fisher and Frey so nicely put it, "Knowing that six or seven students understand [i.e., those who raise their hands] is not the same as knowing that 32 do" (p. 37). Like all of the researchers I cite here, Fisher and Frey are convinced that these elements belong in virtually every lesson but they are *only rarely employed in most classrooms.*

Marilyn Burns

More students fail in math than in any other subject. This has a horrific and disproportionate impact on high school graduation rates and college prospects (Singham, 2005; Steen, 2007). But note Dylan Wiliam's (2007) happy calculation that if we merely implemented the elements of effective lessons routinely, *the United States would move up into the top five in international rankings in math.*

Respected math educator Marilyn Burns emphasizes precisely the same methods advocated by all of the researchers described here.

Successful lessons, she writes, must be taught in planned steps in which the teacher models learning and thinks aloud, followed by opportunities for students to practice. When checks for understanding reveal confusion from any student, the teacher should "stop, deal with the confusion and *move on only when all students are ready*" (2007, p. 18, my emphasis). Students need this support "before they are expected to complete independent work." Echoing Fisher and Frey, Burns urges such methods to ensure a "gradual release to independent work" as students demonstrate mastery (p. 20). She, too, insists that effective lessons include frequent opportunities for *"think-pair-share"* (her emphasis) in which students "explain their math knowledge verbally" as the teacher notes their level of understanding and adjusts instruction accordingly (pp. 18–19).

Robert Marzano

Robert Marzano, whose meta-analyses are legendary, gives appropriate credit to the influence of Madeline Hunter in his book *The Art and Science of Teaching* (2007). With fresh language, he makes the case for the importance of having a clear learning goal and of segmenting each chunk of instruction to optimize learning. Between chunks—at strategic stopping points during the lesson—the effective teacher gathers feedback on learning and processes it immediately; this same-day information determines how much additional explanation is needed in the next step of the lesson.

According to Marzano, these simple elements are so indispensable that they deserve to be "routine components of every lesson" (2007, p. 180). They are essential, whether we are learning a science concept, "listening to a lecture or reading a section of text" (p. 34), or learning to write and edit a compare-and-contrast essay. For Marzano, our fidelity to these elements "constitutes the craft knowledge of teaching . . . the infrastructure of effective and ineffective teaching" (p. 176). But for all their value, these components are not routine at all. As Marzano notes, "Teachers tend not to design and implement" these simple features into their lessons *"even though the resources and materials are readily available"* (p. 176, my emphasis).

Bored yet? Don't be, despite the fact these elements of instruction are quite familiar. Because the payoff isn't in knowing these components; the payoff comes from *actually doing them.* What would happen if we did design *and implement* this simple, universally affirmed structure into our lessons? I'll say it again: We would make educational history.

Let's now look at the evidence. If this evidence won't change our priorities, then nothing will.

The Stunning Impact of Effective Lessons

Researcher James Popham is a former colleague of Madeline Hunter's, and his research explicitly supports the same elements of effective lessons recommended here: a plan for delivering a "sequenced set of subskills . . . [in] step by step building blocks" (2008, p. 24).

He reserves special praise for the pivotal element: formative assessment—or checking for understanding, in Hunter's lexicon. Between each "learning progression" in the lesson, effective teaching requires that we collect formal or informal "assessment evidence" to make "informed adjustments." This ensures that the highest possible proportion of students will "master the target curricular aim" (p. 35).

So why—as I will argue—should we suspend all new initiatives until checking for understanding is consistently implemented in our schools in almost every lesson? For the simple reason that the effects of formative assessment on learning are "among *the largest ever reported*" (p. 2, my emphasis).

Popham is referring to research by Dylan Wiliam (2007), whose work demonstrates the folly of our current priorities, such as investing heavily in technology when it has had, so far, such limited impact on student learning. Like me, Wiliam is dismayed by the parade of popular initiatives and trainings into which we pour time and money while our most effective, least expensive interventions are left at the curb.

He advocates, instead, for the same simple procedures we've been looking at, such as checking for understanding using dry-erase boards or hand signals for students to let teachers know if they are or aren't ready to move on. Just as Pfeffer and Sutton found that old, simple principles are the real drivers of improvement, Wiliam believes the principles that inform the elements of effective lessons have been with us for "thousands of years" (2007, p. 189).

The following evidence should convince us that such simple, old components of effective teaching should be our highest priority—at least until they are satisfactorily implemented by the majority of teachers. Lessons that include effective use of formative assessment and checks for understanding

• Would have *20 to 30 times* as much positive impact on learning than the most popular current initiatives.
• Are about *10 times* as cost-effective as reducing class size.
• Would add between *6 and 9 months* of additional learning growth per year.
• Account for as much as 400 percent "speed of learning differences"; students would learn *four times as fast* as a result of its consistent use (Wiliam, 2007, p. 186).

Impact like this helps explain the findings, cited earlier, that seem too fantastic to believe:

• Only *three years* of effective teaching will catapult students in the lowest quartiles into the third or even fourth quartile (Haycock, 2003).
• Effective teaching could eliminate the achievement gap in about five years (Kain & Hanushek in Schmoker, 2006).

• The highest-performing teachers ensure that students learn twice as much material in the same amount of time as their peers (Garnaut, 2007).

And it explains the recent research findings by Teach for America alluded to earlier. When asked to find what "concrete actions" made the biggest difference in a "lesson plan," Teach for America was surprised to discover that one simple factor accounted for student success more than any other. The best teachers

> Frequently check for understanding: Are the kids—all of the kids—following what you are saying? Asking "Does anyone have any questions?" does not work. (Ripley, 2010, p. 5)

In view of such evidence, how much longer can any self-respecting profession go on pursuing new, complex initiatives every year while ignoring the manifest under-implementation of what is truly effective? *Is it too much to suggest that we declare a temporary moratorium on all new initiatives until this game-changing lesson structure is fully understood and consistently implemented by professional educators in any given school—perhaps in all schools?*

Let's now look at some real teachers who routinely employ the simplest forms of checking for understanding to ensure high-quality learning *and* high test scores for all.

When Teachers Truly Use Formative Assessment

As you take in these brief profiles, keep in mind that these educators' successes were in no way attributable to the use of complicated new strategies, technology, or specious attempts to group students by "learning styles" or ability. Rather, they were all about effective, whole-class teaching in classrooms with a considerable range of levels.

A Primary Grade Reading Teacher

I have been fortunate to know and observe several highly effective kindergarten and 1st grade teachers working in high-poverty schools. Their students learn to read two to three times as fast as their peers, often outperforming the affluent schools in their respective districts.

Their secret is that they spend far less time than their peers attempting to tutor multiple individuals or small groups while most of the students sit passively, waiting for their turn to learn (Ford & Opitz, 2002). From day one, these teachers prefer to provide well-organized, whole-class lessons (which I'll detail in Chapter 4), replete with continuous checks for understanding. That's why virtually all of their students can read within a few short months and can read and decode independently well before the end of the 1st grade.

Kristie Webster, whom I have already mentioned, works at J. B. Sutton Elementary School in inner-city Phoenix. One hundred percent of this school's students receive free or reduced-price lunch. Sutton's scores have soared in the last two years because all teachers now provide whole-class lessons where checks for understanding are consistently employed and monitored. In Webster's 5th grade class, her inner-city charges write daily and read about 40 chapter books per year. Last year, 100 percent of her students passed the state writing exam; 92 percent passed in reading. At Sutton, the principal sits down with each grade-level team once a month to discuss common assessment results and to ensure that the curriculum is being faithfully implemented. (Again, this simple routine is an indispensable leadership practice; see DuFour and others in Schmoker, 2006, pp. 129–137.)

Middle School English Teachers

Two English teachers at a middle school in Arizona spent a day—just one day—revamping their teaching around a simple formula: effective whole-class instruction in reading, discussion, and writing. All students read, discussed, and wrote argumentative papers about the *same readings*. Their lessons were models of step-by-step instruction and formative assessment. I saw, up close, that virtually every student succeeded on every major assessment (which assessed both skillful reading and effective writing, as most papers should). That very year, despite their 45 percent free and reduced-price lunch rate, the teachers' students rose from average to the highest achievers in the state—in a three-way tie with two of the most affluent schools in the state.

High School Social Studies Teacher

An Advanced Placement (AP) Social Studies teacher I know worked in a high-poverty high school across town from his district's affluent sister school. The majority of his simple lessons were models of "interactive lecture" (which we'll examine in a moment): whole-class lecture and note-taking, punctuated by frequent opportunities for students to pair, share, and process their learning. He was always circulating, listening as students discussed, and checking for understanding to ensure they were taking good notes as he adjusted his instruction on this basis. As a result, almost twice as many of his students took and passed the AP History exam as in his affluent sister school.

Another high school teacher, who I've already mentioned, is Sean Connors, who provided very ordinary but effective lessons that always included careful modeling, the use of exemplars (for any writing lesson), and lots of think, pair, and share with continuous checks for understanding and adjustment of instruction. His preferred technology? An overhead projector. His teaching alone caused achievement on the state writing test to surge upward by 26 points—the largest gain by an entire high school, statewide (Schmoker, 2006).

Are we ready to redirect our time and leadership efforts away from the initiative of the month and toward the consistent implementation of sound curriculum delivered by such powerful, "old" instructional methods? One of the best ways to make that happen is for every school and district to create and employ a general lesson template throughout the school and district. Adlai Stevenson High School benefited greatly from the implementation of such a template.

A Common, General Lesson Template at Adlai Stevenson High School

In Chapter 2, I discussed the impressive achievements of Adlai Stevenson High School in Lincolnshire, Illinois. It's of the most successful and celebrated high schools in the United States. Over a period of years, students at the school made immense, uninterrupted gains on every assessment administered—standardized tests, end-of-course and end-of-quarter assessments, and AP exams. The school increased its AP success rate by 800 percent (Schmoker, 2001). Stevenson is a model of effective team-based professional learning communities, where teachers work in teams to ensure that coherent curriculum and effective, ever-improving lessons are consistently implemented. Team-based learning communities are the indispensable structure for both monitoring and ensuring the implementation of common curriculum and effective teaching.

Tim Kanold is the former superintendent and principal of Adlai Stevenson High School, as well as an award-winning teacher and distinguished author of multiple math textbooks. He succeeded Rick DuFour in 2001. Over lunch, we talked about the simple elements of effective teaching that have made such a powerful difference at his school.

At Stevenson, there is a clear, written curriculum for every course, focused on a *severely reduced set of standards* determined by same-course instructors. Of critical importance (as they should be in any effort to improve schooling), there are common end-of-course and end-of-grading-period assessments, the results of which help teachers to make adjustments to instruction—and allow leaders to monitor the implementation of the common curriculum. Importantly, as Kanold shared with me, not more than 20 percent of the common assessments can be multiple choice. The other 80 percent must consist of written responses in the form of explanation, interpretation, and problem solving.

This brings us to *how* teachers teach at Adlai Stevenson. To ensure consistency and to reinforce the essential elements of good lessons, teachers work from a common lesson format that explains precisely those features described here. As Kanold explains, lessons are to be taught in *small steps*. For instance, in a math lesson, teachers *model* only one or two problems, then they *stop* and let students *practice* only those one or two problems while the teacher *circulates*. There should *be at least four or five such cycles* in any class period.

There they are: the small steps, the modeling, and most important, the multiple cycles of guided practice informed, throughout, by checks for understanding. For Kanold, this "real-time, same-day" formative assessment is the heart of an effective lesson. I was particularly struck by his next comments: "We don't want to see the teacher at their desk. You can't check for understanding if you are sitting down. Wherever I go, as a consultant, it seems like *90 percent of teachers are in this habit of spending too much time sitting during the period.*"

Kanold confirms what so many of us see in so many classrooms: that too much sitting and not enough circulating prevents us from knowing if students are on task and actually learning what we are teaching.

All of Kanold's remarks reflect the priority he gave to ensuring the consistent implementation of effective teaching and the central importance of checking for understanding. At Stevenson, this is "one of the primary things we look for when we tour classrooms as a team.* Then we report back on what we saw."

Before we pursue new methods or programs or initiatives that consume huge amounts of precious time and money, we should focus on more deserving priorities: ensuring that a coherent curriculum is in place and being taught in schools where the essential elements of teaching are indeed routine components of every lesson.

Two Simple Templates for Lecture and Literacy Lessons

At this point, I want to apply the basic lesson structure we've been considering to two unoriginal but versatile templates. Together, these overlapping templates could be the basis for effectively teaching 80 percent or more of the curriculum (as they now are in some schools and classrooms, with good results). Because they can be applied so widely, a focus on these would have commensurately wide benefits across the curriculum—and save planning time.

As you'll see, the templates are simple enough for teams to implement immediately, while refining their execution over time. I will be referring to both templates throughout the four subject area chapters.

The templates reflect the following strategies:

---

*As I've written elsewhere, I regard such tours as indispensable. They should be conducted by at least two people who then report on all-school patterns of growth or need for improvement. I am less enthused about walkthroughs as a primary way to provide individual teachers with feedback that they aren't always ready to accept. (I would only do this as a last, not first, resort, though many have done this quite successfully.)

• **Interactive lecture and direct teaching,** where the focus is on the teacher's words and directions, but students take part in lots of pair-sharing, note-taking, or quick-writing.

• **Literacy-based lessons (read, talk, and write) with a focus on any text,** which requires more lengthy treatment and would be used more often than the lecture template in most subjects.

If we implement such templates even reasonably well, around a reasonably coherent common curriculum in each course, we will never have to worry about changes in state or federal standards or assessment. Such lessons will satisfy the demands of any standardized test and, more importantly, will ensure that all students receive an education that prepares them for college, career, and citizenship. Teacher teams, working in team-based professional learning communities, should make the use and mastery of both these templates a high priority.

Interactive Lecture and Direct Teaching

• • •

Lecture proves to be a marvel of efficiency, allowing us to cover a lot of ground quickly. [But done improperly,] lecturing becomes a waste of precious classroom time.

Harvey Silver, Richard Strong, and Matthew Perini

• • •

[Interactive lecture] dramatically increases students' understanding of new information across content areas and at every grade level.

Robert Marzano

• • •

Lecture, done wrong, is among the most boring, least effective forms of teaching. Done right, however, it is highly engaging and among the most effective ways to cover generous amounts of content.

Happily, the term "interactive lecture" is gaining traction. At its heart, we find guided practice, formative assessment, and ongoing adjustments to instruction. To get a vivid sense of how even very straightforward versions of this kind of lecture can have an enormous impact, let's look at some success stories from universities. Professors are discovering that interactive lecture can ensure success for all, even in very challenging courses.

Formative Assessment Goes to College

At Ohio State University, physics professors began to use increasingly popular "clicker" technology, which allows the professor to conduct ongoing checks for understanding. These formative assessment data allow them to make adjustments to the pace of the lecture and to clarify difficult concepts before moving on.

The results have been dramatic. Students in the classes using formative assessment *perform a full letter grade better than those in classes without it*. In addition, the previously large gap between male and female achievement in physics has been eliminated (*Science Daily,* 2008). Last year, the entire Ohio State football team received *A*s in physics because of this technology. (OK, I made that up.)

At Harvard, physics professor Eric Mazur was used to blaming student failure in his physics courses on indolence or inability (sound familiar?)—until, that is, he began to check for understanding by punctuating his lectures with opportunities for students to solve one or two short problems, alone or in pairs. He would then ask them for their answers, which they would give either by a show of hands or by using the clicker technology. If fewer than 90 percent of his students understood the material, he would stop and have them pair up to justify their answers for each other. As they talked, Mazur would circulate, listening for insights that allowed him to address misconceptions immediately, before moving on to the next step or chunk of his lesson.

His methods, like those at Ohio State, had a dramatic and immediate impact on learning that was not lost on Mazur's colleagues. They soon adopted his methods and realized the same kinds of gains. Success rates in physics now hover around 95 percent, and the gap between the highest- and lowest-scoring subgroups has dramatically narrowed.

Perhaps the most promising finding was that interactive lecture and the simplest versions of formative assessment *work for anyone*. They increase achievement independent of the personality of the instructor (Mazur, 1997).

This is "interactive lecture." Again: when something this simple and readily available can have this much immediate, game-changing impact, shouldn't its implementation be given our highest priority in both college and K–12 classrooms?

Interactive Lecture in K–12

Many have contributed to the compelling case for the elements of such interactive lecture in K–12 education. Let's look now at two especially clear sources of information about how to execute it successfully.

In their book *The Strategic Teacher*, Silver, Strong, and Perini (2007) provide a helpful description of "interactive lecture." Echoing Hunter, they recommend that the lecture begin with an "anticipatory" step—with a "hook," a question, or a link to previous learning (p. 25). They go on to describe two good lectures they observed. One was focused on the topic of sectionalism in U.S. history; the other was a 2nd grade lesson on how to write effective sentences. In both cases, the teacher began the lesson with some background information followed by questions to establish purpose and stimulate curiosity (note how both questions are forms of argument that require us to make inferences and draw conclusions):

- **Sectionalism:** How did we go from the Era of Good Feelings in the 1820s to a period of such deep division and disunity in the ensuing years?
- **Effective sentences:** Which of the following sentences is most effective?

After students had a chance to respond to the question, by writing and then talking in pairs, the teacher called on a few of them randomly to "check for understanding"—to see if they understood the task or if they needed additional instruction before moving to the next steps in the lecture.

Small Steps and Guided Practice

Silver, Strong, and Perini describe how the next few activities are delivered in *small, ordered steps*, between which students "practice" with new knowledge by talking, writing (often in the form of notes), or both. These "periodic thinking reviews" give students the chance to process their learning by "drawing conclusions and making inferences" (identical to the language found in Conley's [2005] intellectual standards). All the while, the teacher is observing and listening to ensure that all students are satisfactorily learning before the teacher moves on to the next part of the lecture (pp. 21–26).

These simple moves are nearly indistinguishable from what Marzano (2009) recommends for lessons where "the teacher intends to present content in the form of a lecture." As Marzano makes so clear, this is a highly effective, versatile mode of teaching: "This process *dramatically* increases students' understanding of new information *across content areas and at every grade level*" (p. 86, my emphasis).

As with any good lesson, it is critical that the information in the lecture should be segmented into "chunks" or "small digestible bites" (p. 87). Good lessons respect the limits of memory and the average attention span; importantly, learners need the chance to process new information *every few minutes.*

The Five-Minute Limit

If we want all kids to learn and enjoy that learning, we simply can't lecture for long, uninterrupted periods of time. To this end, both Marzano and Silver, Strong, and Perini are emphatic about time limits between segments of a lecture. Silver, Strong, and Perini recommend that the teacher talk *for "no more than five minutes"* before giving students an opportunity to process the new information—to write or to interact with their peers on the stated learning goal (Silver et al., 2007, p. 23). Similarly, in Marzano's (2009) example, he suggests that after only a few minutes of lecture, students should be given the opportunity to digest or discuss the information they have learned or the notes they have taken. Every few minutes, we should let students process the new learning by

- Reviewing their notes and adding any new insights or connections,
- Summarizing their learning in the last segment of the lecture, or
- Pairing up to compare or contrast notes, perceptions, and connections.

Failure to give students these opportunities is what makes most lectures boring and ineffective. Without these, it is a long, dull day, one we would never wish on ourselves. If we want all students to learn, they need frequent opportunities to talk, write, share, and compare their thoughts.

These processes themselves—taking notes, reviewing notes, and summarizing—must themselves be *taught and modeled regularly* using the same elements of teaching discussed in the last chapter. Teachers should monitor and provide guidance in these all year, every year. Importantly, these processing moments are also opportunities to check for understanding.

Checking for Understanding and Engagement

Stopping points allow teaching to formatively monitor and assess learning (and on-task behavior) by calling on random students and walking around the room to listen and review their notes. During lecture, we must be, as Marzano writes, "continually checking for student understanding" (2009, p. 87). If students are confused or do not understand the content in a particular chunk, the teacher should revisit or reteach that information before moving on to another chunk. Again, I especially like Marzano's insistence that we must ensure, as we lecture, that all are engaged—not just those who raise their hands. We must ensure that *every student* is responding, multiple times, to questions throughout the lecture.

We might be struck by how slow this process seems. But, as noted earlier, such "slow," interactive teaching can account for as much as "400 percent speed of learning differences" and an additional six to nine months of learning growth per year (Wiliam, 2007, p. 186). This process *"dramatically increases* students' understanding of new information across content areas and at every grade level" (Marzano, 2009, p. 87).

In sum, interactive lecture can be a "marvel of efficiency" (Silver et al., 2007, p. 26). It can promote learning for all like few other lessons in our repertoire. Variations on it could constitute a sizeable proportion of the curriculum—with enormous leverage for improvement. Moreover, it can be effective regardless of the personality of the teacher (Mazur, 1997). Therefore, its mastery and the continuous refinement of its execution should be among the team's and school's highest priorities.

The next template is equally if not more powerful and versatile: a simple template for literacy-based lessons in every subject area and grade level.

A Template for Authentic Literacy

• • •

Think of literacy as a spine; it holds everything together. The branches of learning connect to it, meaning that all core content teachers have a responsibility to teach literacy.

Vicki Phillips and Carina Wong

• • •

For all the value in interactive lecture and direct teaching, perhaps the largest proportion of the curriculum should be built around authentic literacy activities in every subject area. The simple, age-old template I'll describe here consists of the following three parts, usually, but not always, in this order:

- Close reading/underlining and annotation of text.
- Discussion of the text.
- Writing about the text informed by close reading, discussion, or annotation.

For centuries, the above activities have been the heart of both *what* we learn and *how* we learn, the key to acquiring both the knowledge and intellectual acumen that transform lives and overcome poverty like no other factor. But as I attempted to demonstrate in *Results Now,* the use and implementation of these simple, authentic literacy activities are among the lowest operative priorities in most schools. A mountain of evidence and classroom observation data proves this (Schmoker, 2006).

Ironically, 30 years of school innovation have had the bizarre consequence of driving authentic literacy underground and supplanting it almost to extinction. Kelly Gallagher's term "readicide" (the murder of reading) aptly captures this phenomenon (Gallagher, 2009). So does the following trenchant observation by Jacqueline Ancess, on yet another lavishly funded, over-hyped reform. After several corporations and thousands of schools had invested in a failed program, she lamented that students in these schools were given no opportunity

> to compose, *write, [or] revise extended analytical papers*. They have never been required to *analyze ideas from multiple perspectives and reach thoughtful conclusions supported by compelling evidence*. They could recall little opportunity to *discuss and debate ideas* . . . they had never built the habit of getting to *engage material to make meaning from it: struggling through text, figuring it out.* (2008, p. 48, my emphasis)

In other words, real students in thousands of schools were *denied an education* as reformers tinkered with school structure. Like every other reform, this one forgot that intensive amounts of reading and writing are the soul of learning. It forgot that learning of the most complex kind is acquired through old-fashioned, simple activities like meaningful reading and writing.

In an ideal world, all aspiring school reformers would be required to read Ancess's lament and sign a binding agreement that they would not let this happen again. As I write this, one of the popular 21st century organizations is advancing a set of "standards" that would supplant meaningful reading and writing activities with having students make websites, video movie trailers, clay animation figures, wikis, sound tracks, and posters—each reflecting students' "individual personalities." These are hugely seductive, multiday activities that sound so much more interesting to some teachers than the authentic literacy activities they would replace.

The lesson to be learned from the last 30 years should be this: We will never educate all students until we appreciate the value of time and stop preventing them from engaging in (by current standards) immense amounts of reading, discussion, and writing. These are the indispensable and primary means of acquiring content knowledge and intellectual skills even—and especially—in the digital age (Phillips & Wong, 2010; Wineburg & Martin, 2004).

The following template is utterly unoriginal, expanding on three activities that have always been at the center of education—close reading, discussion, and writing. They are so rich and so versatile that they could be the basis for most of the curriculum without ever getting stale. (Indeed, these are the basis for perhaps 90 percent of lessons in many seminar-based courses.) This template can be used with reading and writing assignments for portions of any science textbook or novel, critiques of works of music or art, poems, primary historical resources, and magazine articles and newspaper editorials.

In the next few pages, I will explain and add to these three activities to make them clearer and more accessible to educators. But even these additions are merely extensions of reading, discussion, and writing, combined with the elements of any effective lesson (formalized by Madeline Hunter).

Again: There's nothing original here. This basic approach is older than Socrates and is the substance of many college—but precious few high school—courses. This approach constitutes about 90 percent of the daily lessons in the two-hour humanities block at Tempe Preparatory Academy, mentioned earlier. It is the daily diet of instruction in every course at places like St. John's College, Sarah Lawrence College, Oxford University, and Cambridge University. It was the only lesson format used in Cheryl Lockhart's enormously popular English classes at Amphitheater High School in Tucson, Arizona, where I was an employee. Students in Lockhart's class never tired of this seemingly redundant format. They were too busy talking—making inferences, arguing, and weighing the merits of conflicting viewpoints in the various novels, essays, and articles they were reading.

As we briefly review the elements in this template, realize that its effectiveness hinges on the same factors that attract people to book clubs: the chance to acquire knowledge as we read for meaning and express and compare our thoughts and perceptions with others. An entire education can be built on these innately satisfying activities.

Teaching Vocabulary

Before the reading of a text, always be sure to teach any vocabulary that could impede understanding. This simple step can often make a seemingly inaccessible text accessible to all. Learning just a few words or unfamiliar concepts can make a text more accessible by a factor of years—and way more interesting.

Once done, we can move to purpose setting (which overlaps with the concept of anticipatory set).

Establishing a Purpose for the Reading

To create interest in the content of the text, we will want to share some background information about the topic, read an interesting selection from the text, or help students to connect it to recent or previous learning.

Then comes the main event: a question or prompt, linked as often as possible to intellectual skills, such as those Conley (2005) recommends (making inferences/drawing conclusions, analyzing and forming arguments, resolving/synthesizing conflicting opinions, or problem solving). We do these things because students, *regardless of grade level,* will read with greater interest when we get their attention and when we give them a clear, legitimate task or purpose for their reading. For example, author and practicing teacher Kelly Gallagher always gives his students their final exam question *before* they begin reading an assigned novel (2009).

Here are some examples of prompts or questions that establish a purpose for different subject area texts; they also serve as end-of-unit learning targets or writing tasks. All should be posted prominently at the beginning of a lesson or unit and thoroughly clarified before the reading.

- **Science.** Compare and contrast the functions of the digestive and respiratory systems; meiosis and mitosis; the arguments for wind versus solar energy; the case for or against global warming.

- **English.** Make inferences about a character or his/her development, such as Jack in *Jack and the Beanstalk* or Amir in *The Kite Runner* (based on thoughts, words, and actions); identify similarities and differences between two characters—such as Old Dan/Little Anne in *Where the Red Fern Grows*—as you draw inferences about the author's message.

- **Social Studies.** Make arguments for why you would prefer life as a Mayan or an Aztec, or as a U.S. or Canadian citizen, with references to both (using textbooks and current publications).

- **Mathematics.** Argue for which solution to a problem is most complete and accurate; weigh the quantitative arguments in two opposing article(s) about federal spending (e.g., Paul Krugman on the left versus George F. Will on the right).

- **Art/Music.** Compare and contrast or argue the merits of one artist or musician over another, or of two conflicting reviews of an art show or musical performance in a magazine or newspaper.

The quality and availability of good questions is essential to engagement and interest as students read, discuss, and write. Forgive the repetition, but once again I must emphasize: Teams should make the development and refinement of *good text-based questions among their highest priorities*—creating banks of temporary and permanent collections of questions readily available to all teachers, trying the questions, and then discussing results (Which questions worked? Which bombed?).

Once we are sure that students grasp the question (by conducting a brief check for understanding), we then tell them how their work will be assessed. Assessment can be done in any of the following ways:

- A review of students' notes or annotations (done in a quick walk-around, as one of my daughter's English teachers did effectively; students don't need to know when you formally record these for credit).

- Actual writing (which can often be graded quickly, checked off, or scanned).

- Participation in a discussion (see discussion rubric below).

- All three of the above over the course of a multiday lesson or unit, always with an eye to reducing time spent taking home or grading papers. (For more ways to increase writing and greatly reduce grading time, see "Write More, Grade Less" at my website, www.mikeschmoker.com.)

We should get used to the idea that purposeful reading normally requires active processing—whether we have students annotate, jot, take notes, or summarize their thoughts at certain points in the reading. *But we must teach students explicitly how to do such active reading*—routinely, at every grade level, and at least twice a week in every course. It all starts with modeling or "thinking aloud."

Modeling Higher-Order Reading

Any teacher who got through college or has been in a good book club can read critically and annotate. With a little practice, teachers can quickly learn to model such reading. Be confident: *You* are the best reader in the room.

We'll see how to do such modeling in every subject area in Chapters 4 to 7. But for now, let's suppose we are teaching 2nd graders to read *Jack and the Beanstalk* (which I've done many times). After teaching any potentially troublesome vocabulary, we establish purpose by asking an inferential/argumentative question, such as, "What is your opinion of Jack, based on his words and actions? Is he a noble, heroic character—or maybe not?"

Of course, variations on this question can be used with almost any work of fiction or to analyze a political, scientific, or historical figure. Another variation on this assignment would be to have students read the story and then also read—and annotate—copies of two conflicting essays on the story written by former students (with names blacked out). Have students discuss which makes the stronger argument.

Whatever we do, we now need to show students how *we* would read the text, and what we would underline or annotate as we "think aloud." For example, in the first few lines of *Jack and the Beanstalk*, we find that Jack and his mother are very poor and in dire straits. Then Jack says, "Cheer up, Mother, I'll go and get work somewhere." Upon reading this, you might say,

> Well, good for Jack! Don't you think it's admirable for a young boy to look for work to help his family? I'm going to underline that—and maybe write "admirable—so young" in the margin.

But in the very next line of the story, we find that Jack's mother says, "We've tried that before, and nobody would take you." At this point, you might say,

> Whoa . . . why wouldn't anyone "take" Jack—I guess that means they wouldn't hire him? Was it because he was too young? Or maybe he had a reputation as someone who didn't work hard or wasn't very responsible? I don't know yet—but that's OK. I'm hoping that as we read on, we'll find other actions of Jack's that might help answer my question. Remember, students, that even adults have unanswered questions as they read. So let's see what else Jack does and says in the next few paragraphs. Further reading might give us a clearer impression of what kind of person Jack is.

You get the idea.

I can guarantee you, from experience, that any conscientious attempt to model reading in such a fashion will reveal that 2nd graders are *fully up to such truly college-preparatory tasks*. Be ready for it—and prepare to make such reading a routine feature of instruction a few times a week in every subject area.

Frequent modeling of reading, underlining, and annotating, in every course, is critical to accelerating the attainment of core intellectual processes—several years ahead of time. Some won't ever learn to read critically unless we show them how we do such reading several times a week with all kinds of texts, including newspapers or history and science textbooks. We'll see more examples of this in the subject area chapters.

After we model how we would read, underline, annotate, or take notes, students are ready to practice such reading themselves alone, then in pairs—with our guidance.

Guided Practice and Formative Assessment

The next step is to have students practice, by themselves, the same kind of reading, note-taking, or annotation that you've just modeled, with the next paragraph or section of text. As they practice, check for understanding to see if additional clarification or modeling is needed. Here are a few ways to do this:

• **Circulate as students underline, annotate, or take notes.** This is my favorite approach, as a quick one- to two-minute tour will tell you a lot. Are students underlining or taking notes appropriately? If not, you must provide additional modeling or instruction to provide greater clarity.

• **Have students pair up and share.** Students should frequently pair up and share their notes, annotations, or underlined text with each other. Again, talking is not only one of the best ways to digest information, it is also a needed break and a low-threat opportunity for students to get feedback from peers on their ability to read for meaning. Meanwhile, as students pair up, you can circulate, listening to the conversations. (This is not the best time to tutor individual students or groups, which may impede the flow and pace of the lesson.)

- **Call on random pairs to share their thoughts.** This gives students an opportunity to express themselves in a more public mode while also giving you a feel for how ready they are for independent practice and how best to clarify or model the active reading processes in a different way.

- **Ask students to quick-write while you circulate.** Before *or* after students pair up, ask them to quick-write brief explanations, connecting their notes or underlined text to the prompt or question. Remember that any form of writing, short or long, *generates and refines thought.* Quick-writing helps students to "rehearse"— to formulate and articulate their thoughts before they share their insights with a partner or, if the teacher chooses, with the whole class in a larger discussion. I can assure you that there are inestimable benefits to letting students see how their peers read and share perceptions and insights. Again, such interaction mimics the pleasures of a good book club.

Remember to set time limits for the readings, discussions, and writings—or for any of the stages in a lesson. If you don't already do this, try it; it acts powerfully to help students stay focused and on task. If they need more time, give it to them.

Above all, circulate! For all of the above, *at least at crucial times,* walk around for a few minutes and listen, ensure on-task behavior, and scan student work so that you can more precisely guide the next steps of learning and not leave students behind. Do they need you to model some more, to show them how adults often *slow down or reread* to understand certain important or dense sections of text, to help them make connections to the question or prompt, or to model how to collect supporting evidence for their arguments? For all of these, and for as long as we teach, the answer will very often be *yes*.

In due course, these multiple cycles of guided practice and checking for understanding allow for the "gradual release of responsibility" (Fisher & Frey, 2007) for students to complete the assessment/ assignment (often one and the same) independently.

Independent Practice and Assessment

As a result of the previous steps—for any text in any subject area—you should feel roughly confident that students are ready for the next step: to purposefully underline, annotate, or take notes by themselves as they finish reading texts. Of course, if students practice these routines a couple of times a week in several courses, fewer iterations will be required before they are ready to finish reading on their own.

Keep in mind that *students never learn such analytic reading* once and for all. I believe teachers should model and conduct guided practice at the beginning of most reading assignments—at ever higher levels of sophistication and with ever more challenging texts, at every grade level. Independent practice time can also be a good time to work with those few remaining students who might require extra assistance.

Again, *perfect execution of these processes is not required*. The real power of this simple, multipurpose template is in its being done *regularly and frequently*—at least twice a week in most courses, from 2nd grade through senior year. As you practice it and work on its successful use in your team, you will become very good at every part of it.

All of the steps discussed so far are immensely valuable by themselves. But they are also invaluable as "rehearsals" for each of the following two steps: whole-class discussion/debate, followed by some form of writing. The close reading, annotating, and quick-writes will build students' confidence and ability to participate in these activities with newfound confidence and skill—and even, as you'll discover, enthusiasm.

Whole-Class Discussion and Debate

People truly do enjoy sharing what they have learned from close reading. Do our teachers know the findings of an ASCD survey that asked students how they like to learn? Eighty-three percent of them indicated that "discussion and debate" was a method that would "excite them most" (Azzam, 2008). How often are the rudiments of effective discussion—and its immense appeal for students—taught in preservice training or reinforced in staff development and faculty meetings (which ought to be among our primary staff development opportunities)? How often do we reward and recognize the successful use of classroom discussion?

Believe me: Once students have had the benefit of close reading, annotating, and partner-sharing, they will be eager to discuss and debate issues they find in their textbooks, historical documents, and editorials, or in print and online publications like *TIME for Kids*. For example, students might debate topics like these:

• The pros and cons of T. Boone Pickens's "Plan for Energy Independence" (there is a lot of very readable stuff on this available on the Internet).

• Healthcare legislation—good or bad policy?

• President Obama's 2008 Philadelphia speech justifying his relationship to the Reverend Wright. Most of the speech is very interesting because it's so personal, and it is very readable by upper elementary students.

• President Lincoln's second inaugural address. Would it be conciliatory or inflammatory to the average Southerner of the time?

• Jay Gatsby's character: Should we sympathize with him (as a victim of the culture of the 1920s) or condemn him for the tragic events in *The Great Gatsby*?

We'll see plenty of additional examples of such interesting topics and texts in the coming chapters.

We greatly underestimate both the educational power and enjoyment students derive from such discussions or debates, if they are adequately prepared for them by the steps described above. But to get the most out of discussion, we should establish clear criteria for productive participation.

Remember that a good discussion is not a free-for-all; it should be tied directly to the posted learning goal or question and follow simple procedures that should be explicitly taught and reinforced like any good lesson.

To become good listeners and communicators, students need modeling, guided practice, and formative assessment as they learn to meet criteria such as the following:

- Always cite the text when making an argument.
- When disagreeing with another's conclusions, argument, or solutions, briefly restate what they said, don't interrupt, and be civil and respectful.
- Be concise and stay on point.
- Avoid distracting verbal tics (such as overuse of "like" or "you know").

This kind of brief rubric could be enough (less is more). But if we want students to become clear, articulate speakers, all of the above must be demonstrated, modeled, and reinforced by the teacher throughout discussions. (If these are consistently reinforced throughout the school, the benefits will be compounded.)

I don't think we can overestimate the value of such discussions. I recently observed a Socratic discussion at Tempe Preparatory Academy (in a chemistry class, of all places). I was deeply impressed by how the habit of such regular discussions in most of the school's classes had made the students into such poised, confident, and effective speakers and listeners. The conversation was so engaging that students stayed after the bell rang.

A nice variation might be the "fishbowl" discussions recommended by assessment expert Rick Stiggins (1994), where an outside ring of students observes and evaluates the discussion shared among the students in the inner ring. This strategy could greatly enhance students' discussion skills.

Discussion skills are critical in every sphere and as preparation for individual presentations. They are not only for the college-bound or the gifted; they are for *all* students, who deserve to participate in them regularly—at least twice a week in most courses (more on this in the subject area chapters).

Fortunately, effective text-based reading and discussion are, in turn, *the perfect preparation for writing*—which takes thinking to an even higher level. More than perhaps any other activity, writing enhances students' ability to think, make connections, and achieve clarity, logic, and precision. Writing enables us to discern and then express critical distinctions between truth and half-truth, between good sense and attractive nonsense. Enormous power attaches to those who *do* write and *can* write (Graff, 2003; National Commission on Writing, 2003).

Student Writing, with Reference to the Text

I won't be exhaustive or overly prescriptive here; you'll find more detail in the subject area chapters. And you could modify or rearrange some of the steps I'll describe.

Writing, from short scribbles to more formal pieces, profits from the previous processes of close reading, annotation, and discussion of one or more texts. Armed with these understandings, students should return to the text and do the following:

• Quietly review and re-read their notes, underlinings, or annotations to decide which they will write about and which would best serve the purpose of the assignment (to argue, draw conclusions, problem solve, reconcile or synthesize conflicting views).

- Arrange or organize the best of these thoughts, quotes, and data into a quick list or formal outline.

Then, they write.

Across the curriculum, the majority of writing assignments would be just this simple. Frequency is paramount, but most of these almost-daily assignments *don't need to be formally graded—* only completed, checked off, or given credit if a quick glance reveals them to be an honest attempt to cite the text and respond appropriately to a question or prompt. Some assignments might be evaluated, in less or more depth, for content and clarity. Others—in language arts—could be evaluated for the finer points of composition and mechanics.

Modeling of such writing is critical here as well. Teachers have to "think aloud" to demystify how to select the best quotes, facts, and data; how to make lists and outlines; and how, for more formal assignments, to make adjustments during the prewriting and writing process.

In English and language arts, however, teachers do have to ensure that students get more detailed writing instruction, including instruction in all the elements of a good writing rubric (more on this in the next chapter). We will revisit the more minimalist writing and scoring requirements for social studies, science, and math in later chapters.

In all subjects, but especially in language arts, teaching will be greatly enhanced and learning will be accelerated by having students analyze exemplar papers written by students or professionals. *Nothing enhances the power of a writing lesson like an actual example;* students need to see how good writers organize their arguments, write effective sentences, and choose appropriate language.

Because most categories of good persuasive/expository writing have the same basic elements, you can often use the same exemplar paper for multiple assignments if you wish to, as you build your "permanent collection." Every teacher team, in every subject, should have a good collection of papers for this purpose.

Finally, in any subject where you assign a formal paper, you would be smart to "vet" students' theses and outlines before they plunge deeply into the work (Jago, 2005). (Carol Jago's book also has good practical tips on writing and on time-efficient grading practices.) As a teacher, I found this to have tremendous benefits for me and my students. It is a critical but oft-neglected stage in instruction for helping students learn to get their arguments and support organized. It saves them precious time and frustration (and thus keeps from developing an aversion to writing). And it saves teachers time grading. A focused, well-organized argumentative paper is always easier to grade and a more positive, productive experience for students. (Again, for more on this and other ways to avoid the "paper load," see "Write More, Grade Less" at www.mikeschmoker.com.)

• • •

Throughout the next few chapters, I will be referring to the two templates discussed here, variations on which could be used countless times per year in any discipline while assuring that students' skills in critical reading, thinking, speaking, and writing will advance apace. Bet on it.

Used right, the templates directly address the essential intellectual skills described by David Conley (2005): the ability to read for inference, analyze and synthesize conflicting viewpoints, support argument with evidence, and solve open-ended problems.

Any teacher can begin implementing and refining the use of the two templates in team-based professional learning communities. If we learned and implemented them in conjunction with a coherent curriculum, students would receive an education that equips them, like never before, for the rigors and pleasures of contributive citizenship, careers, or college.

Let's now look at *what* and *how* we should teach in four subject areas, with a strong emphasis on literacy. The implications for any discipline should be readily apparent.

SECTION II

Curriculum, Instruction, and
Literacy in the Content Areas

4

English Language Arts
Made Simple

Adolescents entering the adult world of the 21st century will read and write more than at any other time in human history. They will need advanced levels of literacy to perform their jobs, run their households, act as citizens, and conduct their personal lives.

Richard Vacca

• • •

The explosion of media and technology . . . has made it all the more important that students master the core skills of gathering and evaluating evidence. Reading and writing with independence and confidence will remain master arts in the information age.

Vicki Phillips

• • •

Literature makes significant life possible. . . . [We] construct ourselves from novels, poems, and plays as well as from works of history and philosophy.

Mark Edmundson

Language arts, more than any discipline, has lost its way. It is in desperate need of clarity. To that end, we need to simplify and reconceive English language arts standards. Without meaning to, state standards and assessments have had a uniquely destructive effect here. As currently conceived, they have corrupted language education and its essential mission: to ensure that students can read, write, and speak effectively in and out of school. New, smarter standards would clarify literacy and ensure something current standards (including the national standards) don't adequately address: that every year, *every student needs to spend hundreds of hours actually reading, writing, and speaking for intellectual purposes.*

In this chapter, I'll advocate for a very simple model of both *what* and *how* we teach in English language arts, starting in the primary grades. I will make frequent references to the literacy template described in Chapter 3. At the end of this chapter, we'll see how three schools assured that their students were spending hundreds of hours reading, writing, and speaking every year.

All disciplines connect and contribute to success in other disciplines. But as we've seen, language competency is the foundation of learning in the other disciplines. As McConachie and colleagues aver, students "develop deep conceptual knowledge in a discipline only by using the habits of *reading, writing, talking and thinking,* which that discipline values and uses" (2006, pp. 8–14).

Many of us know E. D. Hirsch for his ardent advocacy of content knowledge in the disciplines. As we saw earlier, that hasn't prevented him from concluding that literacy is "the most important single goal of schooling"—a reliable indicator of general competence and life chances (2010, p. 1). Language arts matters greatly in every subject area—a fact that the national standards quite formally (and admirably) recognize. If we can get this discipline right, the benefits will be amplified throughout the curriculum.

It all starts with reading.

The Life-Changing Power of Broad, Abundant Reading

• • •

If you're born poor, you'd better start reading.

Joe Queenan

Here is a simple fact: Wide, abundant reading is the surest route out of poverty and the limitations that impose themselves on the less literate. *Reading changes everything.* According to Jacques Barzun, "No subject of study is more important than reading . . . all other intellectual powers depend on it" (1991, p. 21). Or, as Aldous Huxley wrote, "Every man who knows how to read has it in his power to magnify himself, to multiply the ways in which he exists, to make his life full, significant and interesting."

Rafe Esquith is a bestselling author and 5th grade teacher in high-poverty East Los Angeles. Esquith knows how much depends on the ability to read well. He writes:

> Let's face it: reading is the most important subject in school. It's more important than all the other subjects combined. (2003, p. 30)

> I want my students to know that their ability to read and write is a matter of life and death. (p. 44)

It is only logical—isn't it?—that Esquith shuns basal readers and skills exercises so that his students can read abundantly and intensely. (We'll look at his ambitious reading list, which *all of his students* read, in a moment.) As a result of Esquith's unorthodox curriculum, hundreds of his students "leave his 5th grade classroom and go on to accomplish remarkable things" (Esquith, 2003, p. 30). His students perform at the 91st percentile; the average in the rest of his school is in the 40s.

Why this heartbreaking and unnecessary difference? Because the rest of his school, like the overwhelming majority of schools, doesn't fully understand the value of simply reading, deeply and broadly, for hours every week in class. Instead of reading and talking and writing about lots of fiction and nonfiction books and other documents, Esquith's fellow teachers—urged on by their "reading coaches"—prefer to use basal readers and skills worksheets (Esquith, 2003, p. 30).

When will we learn, in the words of Esquith's aptly named book, that *there are no shortcuts*? School improvement is impossible without ensuring that students read abundantly—for hundreds of hours, every year. Hundreds of hours? Of course; let's not forget we have about 1,000 hours per year to work with. Surely we can devote 20 percent or more of that time to reading—with plenty of time left over for discussing and writing and teaching generous amounts of content in every discipline.

Let's now look at the kinds of texts that students should be reading in abundance, and why each is so vital to their education and empowerment. We'll begin with literature—key to a life that is "full, significant, and interesting."

Reading Literature

No one writes better on the uses of literature than Mark Edmundson (2004), a professor of English at the University of Virginia. He knows how literature should be taught, how it enlarges us and allows us to inhabit and evaluate the lives and worldviews of others as we reflect on our own. "Reading," he writes, "woke me up. It took me from a world of harsh limits into expanded possibility" (p. 1). Through literary studies, he found that his very "consciousness had been expanded" (p. 4).

Edmundson wants all students to have this experience. For this to happen, he offers an essential corrective: Literature is not primarily about "figuring out" symbolism or figurative language or setting or mood or structure. These are absurdly overemphasized in state standards—as they are in the new national standards. They are secondary, if not tertiary, matters. Literature is primarily about us, as individuals, as people seeking to understand ourselves and the world we share. Unfortunately, fiction is too often taught as though it is an abstract game or code.

Literature is something much simpler, more direct, and more personal: an opportunity to weigh our own values and emotional resonance against those of the author and the characters he or she creates. Do we like, dislike, relate to, or learn from the characters or the author's implicit messages? Do we see ourselves, or our culture, or people we know more clearly as a result of our encounters with fictional characters from near or far, past or present? This is and has always been the primary pleasure and purpose of reading literature, plays, poetry, or memoirs. The rest is largely ornamentation.

Literature allows us to reflect, to recognize the subtle ideas and forces operating in our own lives—and thus to shape them. Edmundson describes the personal epiphany of one of his students, a college athlete, while reading *The Iliad*. She suddenly saw herself in Achilles. In reading about his single-minded focus on victory and dominance, she realized she had never consciously reflected on the value of such an obsession—her own—or its effects on other areas of her life. Was Achilles someone to emulate? Why? The experience was deeply personal and transformative. The new national reading standards have some good points, but they barely touch on this, the simple essence of the literary experience and literary studies.

Literature, art, and poetry enlarge us and refine our values and sensibilities. Through them, writes Edmundson (2004), we are able to uncover and refine our "central convictions about politics, love, money, the good life" (p. 28). As Kelly Gallagher (2009) writes,

> I am a different person because I have read *1984*. I see my government differently, I consider privacy issues differently and I have a heightened sense of propaganda and language manipulation—all because I have read this novel. (p. 57)

I, too, am a different person, as are many of you, because of the characters and ideas I have encountered in prose and poetry. The same is true of the ideas and characters we encounter in nonfiction, literary nonfiction, and current news and opinion articles. These enlarge us as well, and they allow us to acquire the knowledge essential to critical thinking.

Nonfiction and Literary Nonfiction

As we saw earlier, Willingham (2009b) found that content knowledge and critical thinking are inseparable and reciprocal. And what is the best way to acquire such knowledge? Books themselves play an indispensable role. Reading "[b]ooks expose[s] children to more facts and to a broader vocabulary (a form of knowledge) than *any other activity*" (p. 37, my emphasis).

Nonfiction books are among the richest sources of knowledge. I wholly agree with Will Fitzhugh (2006) that K–12 requirements should greatly increase the number of whole, nonfiction books students read, not just excerpts (see also Mathews, 2010).

English class is the primary place where we should ensure that students read and acquire an appetite for content-rich nonfiction books. Biographies and memoirs, the most prominent form of literary nonfiction, can be among the richest sources of knowledge. But books are not enough. Willingham adds elsewhere that students also acquire essential knowledge and thinking skills "through years of exposure to newspapers, serious magazines . . . from a content-rich curriculum in school" (Willingham, 2009a, p. 2).

I am convinced, and will argue in each of the remaining chapters, that an engaging, content-rich curriculum must include frequent, meaningful, in-class opportunities to read and discuss newspapers and serious magazines in every subject from the earliest grades.

Newspapers and Magazines in the Classroom

Contrary to what some assume, students enjoy current issues and events, especially when they are framed in controversy. I have seen the most indifferent students talk and write with enthusiasm when asked to read and exchange opinions about controversial issues and people such as off-shore drilling, Sarah Palin, and President Obama.

For years, I have recommended that teachers set aside about one day a week to read current articles and opinion pieces, especially in English, social studies, and science (Schmoker, 2006, pp. 170–172). Author and high school teacher Kelly Gallagher actually does this. He calls it "Article of the Week." He started when he discovered that only a few of his high school students could name the current vice president. They also thought that "Al Qaeda" was a guy named "Al" (2009, p. 28). (To see a full year of "Articles of the Week" used at Gallagher's school, go to www.kellygallagher.org.)

We should redouble our efforts to integrate current readings into the curriculum. If we can get students interested in the issues of their own time (and we can), they will be far more interested in issues, people, and literature of the past.

Current events animate student interest in literature, politics, and history. The new norm should be something like what Gallagher now does when he teaches *All Quiet on the Western Front*: he juxtaposes it with a close reading of two opposing articles on the Iraq war (2009, p. 27). Assembling and organizing such reading materials—with good questions—should be among a teaching team's highest priorities.

There are many good sources available. In the early grades, the *Weekly Reader, TIME for Kids, KidBiz,* and *Junior Scholastic* contain rich, readable news stories for students as young as seven. We should be reading and discussing these for hours every week, instead of continuing to drill students in reading skills (like "adding -ed and -ing ending" to 20 words for half of the period).

Even better, for upper elementary, a surprising amount of adult newspaper, magazine, and opinion pieces can be read and understood if you provide some background and vocabulary (and by using the procedures in the literacy template described in Chapter 3). These same articles can be just as interesting to high school seniors. I collect such articles, and so should professional learning community teams in every discipline. Some might become part of a permanent collection that can be used and shared with other teams, in some cases for years. I have tested various articles from editorial pages, *Newsweek*, and *The Wall Street Journal* on focus groups, asking them the grade levels for which they would be appropriate. The groups invariably concur that the articles could be read and discussed by 5th graders—and would be highly engaging to them.

One of my favorite sources of readable current events articles is *The Week*, a weekly news and opinion magazine. Many of the articles in *The Week* could be read by upper elementary students as well as by high school seniors. These articles are excellent for lessons in how to closely read and annotate (using, as always, repeated modeling, guided practice, and formative assessment). One of my favorite regular features in *The Week* is the "Controversy of the Week." It starts with a summary and is then followed by about six brief summaries of opinion pieces from across the political spectrum—all in about half a page! This is highly readable, interesting stuff, perfect for teaching students to make inferences, draw their own conclusions, argue, problem solve, and reconcile conflicting opinions (Conley, 2005).

I'm looking at one article now, about Joe Wilson's "You lie!" shout-out during one of President Obama's speeches. The piece is written in clear, readable prose. It is packed with facts and implications about related issues—immigration, health care, and race. It even describes historical and global precedents for the incident.

Kids enjoy controversy. Reading and talking about such articles may be the best and fastest way to accelerate the average student's interest in the world and to initiate entry into national and international adult conversation. English teachers need to make serious room for such reading, followed by discussion and writing.

Moreover, such articles make great exemplars for teachers to use when they teach writing.

As Gallagher (2009) writes, "We are what we read," and inversely, "We are what we don't read" (p. 45). If we want all students to learn, the actions we must take are stunningly simple: We must ensure that all students complete hundreds of hours of reading, every year. Large portions of this reading should be done in language arts.

But make no mistake: This amount of reading would entail fundamental changes to language arts standards and instruction. Allow me now to share an extended critique of current standards and curriculum, at both elementary and secondary levels. A breakthrough here would have magnificent consequences for kids.

The Trouble with Skills and Standards

• • •

Read-i-cide n.: the systematic killing of the love of reading, often exacerbated by the inane, mind-numbing practices found in schools.

Kelly Gallagher

• • •

Broad, wide reading is the heart of the language arts. But what else does it lay the groundwork for? I love Mike Rose's simple, ageless formulation: that to become educated, we must primarily read, talk, and write our way toward understanding (Rose, 1989, pp. 32–34). If we want all students to be college-ready, then we must rely on ordinary, redundant routines like those found in the literacy template: having students read closely and purposefully almost daily and then use that reading as the basis for writing and discussion equally frequently.

But first we need to examine how current reading and language arts standards interfere with the acquisition of literacy, in both elementary and secondary schooling. I would argue that many, if not most, of the current language arts standards are not literacy standards at all; they are pseudo-standards that divert precious time and attention from the most simple, authentic kinds of literacy activities.

Skills Kill: The Elementary Years

• • •

The mistaken idea that reading is a skill—learn to crack the code, practice comprehension strategies—may be the single biggest factor holding back reading achievement in the country.

Daniel Willingham

• • •

In the early grades, a typical set of reading standards contains dozens of skills. State standards and popular basal programs have rendered reading into finer and more inane subskills. Teachers now devote precious time to helping students, in tutorials or small groups, to do things like "distinguish between initial, medial or final sounds," "alphabetize a series of words to the 2nd or 3rd letter," or "segment spoken phonemes contained in one syllable words of two to five phoneme sounds into individual phoneme sounds." The national standards (despite some of their merits) are equally as guilty of this: There are far too many of them, and they are ever so prone to be taught with worksheets—the archenemy of abundant, purposeful reading (and discussion and writing).

Very early on, there is a place for phonics, phonemic units, and certain reading skills. But we are guilty of overkill. We teach and test skills and standards to death, into the 3rd and 4th grade. And we lean too hard on the small-group model, which means that students spend about two-thirds of the so-called "reading block" *waiting to learn instead of learning—or actually reading* (Ford & Opitz, 2002).

In the main, we make regrettable use of time in early-grade reading classes. If we changed this, students could be (largely) independent readers by about the middle of the 2nd grade. At that point, they could begin to acquire the knowledge, vocabulary, and thinking skills that will optimize learning in subsequent grade levels. But this can't happen if we continue to unnecessarily elongate a skills-based reading curriculum.

Postponing Reading—and Learning

John Taylor Gatto is a two-time New York state teacher of the year, and he is outraged at typical early-grade reading instruction in public schools. Instead of ameliorating the achievement gap, typical reading instruction perpetuates it.

A keen observer of typical practices and an educational historian, Gatto notes that highly literate societies of the past never had to undergo the inanities of modern reading instruction. He believes public education, despite its good intentions, is culpable here: "One of the central assumptions which allow the institutional school to sustain itself . . . [is] the false assumption that it is difficult to learn to read" (2002, p. xxxvii).

We have indisputable evidence that we could greatly accelerate the process of teaching students to read and decode. As I pointed out in Chapter 3, there are kindergarten and 1st grade teachers in challenging settings who have managed to get almost all of their students reading independently by the middle or end of the 1st grade. Once students begin to read, they learn to read better by reading— just reading—not by being forced to endure more reading skill drills.

The differences that make these teachers so effective are stark and simple: large amounts of their instruction are whole-class, with minimal time spent in ability groups. *This means all students are learning almost all of the time.*

Second, students in effective classrooms never, ever engage in cut, color, or paste activities that now occupy the majority of early-grade reading programs—more than 100 instructional hours per year (Ford & Opitz, 2002).

Third, these teachers obsessively implement the elements of good lessons, with checks for understanding throughout their lessons. I cannot tell you how rarely I observe these elements in early-grade reading classes.

Classrooms That Work: Where Time Is Sacred

In their book *Classrooms That Work: They Can All Read and Write* (2007), Cunningham and Allington note that for the most effective teachers, time is sacred. The highest-performing teachers never waste a minute of class time; there are no arts-and-crafts activities during the reading block. All students are always on task. And what they learn differs markedly from the arcane, irrelevant skills found in early-grade reading standards documents.

In these classrooms, students are immersed in daily extended instruction in very simple, ordinary elements of reading: the alphabet and its sounds, common blends, and irregular spelling patterns—and words, words, words. Whole classes clap, chant, and recite words and syllables chorally, every day. They repeatedly practice and master the 37 most common spelling patterns, the 50 most common transferable word chunks, and—of special importance—high-frequency word lists.

New words are always being learned and recited; they are *written down, multiple times, every day;* they are posted on "word walls" and (important!) referred to incessantly to build up students' reading vocabulary. Students are always reading books along with the teacher, with their fingers on each word. *These simple activities must be done assiduously, with guided practice and checks for understanding, and on an extended and daily basis.* Because if they are done, they will reduce by months or even years the time it takes to learn read independently.

These teachers are successful because this is all they and their students do; they aren't distracted by the skills worksheets and coloring that are so common in classrooms encumbered by the basal programs and the (typically excessive) reliance on the small-group/guided-reading model.

Virtually any student can learn the mechanics of reading to decode grade-level text in about 100 days. That means virtually all could be reading shortly after mid-year of 1st grade (Engelmann, Haddox, & Bruner, 1983). If kindergarten does its part, they may read even earlier. Once they can decode, they only need very small amounts of skills review.

What they *do* need, immediately, are extended daily opportunities to read, much of it for pleasure. When we continue to teach reading skills, we prevent the rapid acquisition of knowledge and vocabulary—at a critical, formative moment in a child's education.

50,000 Words—ASAP!

When we unnecessarily elongate the process of "learning to read," we postpone "reading to learn"—learning itself—by years. It's that simple. Students aren't truly mature readers until they can read and recognize about 50,000 words. *This many words can't be learned by having students sound out, syllabicate, or learn each one.* The only way they can be learned is for us to ensure that they read, by today's standards, enormous, unprecedented amounts of reading material (Smith, 2006, p. 41).

Sadly, the default design of typical K–4 literacy programs reduces actual reading time to a fraction of what students need to acquire vocabulary and become knowledgeable. This is where the seeds of our current literacy crisis are sown. By 4th grade, most students are years behind where all of them *could be* in vocabulary development, general knowledge, and thinking skills.

I marvel, in my travels, at how often I encounter 2nd or 3rd grade students, in very challenged school settings, who clearly can read and decode fluently. Some of them can and do read chapter books at home or for pleasure. But they can't do this at school because they are still being taught *how to read*. Instead of learning skills, they should be reading short and long literary and nonfiction works. By

2nd or 3rd grade, virtually every student could be reading 15 to 20 chapter books per year, some self-selected. If we would just *let them read*, they would acquire unprecedented amounts of knowledge and thousands of vocabulary words. Much of this reading should be for pleasure, with plenty of opportunities to learn to underline and annotate, starting with stories like *Jack and the Beanstalk*. They could be discussing and writing short essays where they argue, infer, and draw their own conclusions about fictional and real-life characters; they could be preparing for college by the 2nd grade.

But we won't let them. Not in the early grades, and not in the later years, when they will encounter an equally irrelevant set of language arts standards. Cumulatively, our wrong-headed emphasis on skills and standards represents what Kelly Gallagher (2009) calls "readicide."

Readicide: When Pseudo-Standards Kill Authentic Literacy

The tendency to conflate reading skills and pseudo-standards with real literacy is lamentable. Of course, the impulse to elongate and prolong the teaching of such skills is encouraged by the textbook industry, which has enjoyed uncritical acceptance and profits from our use of workbooks, worksheets, and (hopelessly banal) reading materials. I sometimes refer to these short books—written expressly to match the least relevant skills—as "factory lit": mass-produced, low-quality reading material. This means, from upper elementary through secondary, students are largely occupied with readings and worksheets built around trivial standards like these:

- Alphabetize to the third letter.
- Drop the final "e" and add "-ing" or "-ed" endings.
- Identify literary terms (such as protagonist, antagonist).
- Identify distinguishing features of nonfiction, plays, short stories, poetry.

- Identify the main idea.
- Distinguish between major and minor characters.
- Identify the proper sequence of events.
- Identify rising action, falling action, and climax in a story.

The national standards would actually have us teaching 4th graders to "form and use the progressive tense (e.g., *I was walking, I am walking, I will be walking*) verb aspects." (Worksheet, anyone?)

Look at the above and ask yourself: Would a regular reader—one who has been taught to purposefully annotate, discuss, and write about plays and poems and nonfiction works from the 2nd grade on—need to be taught to add "-ed" or "-ing" endings to words or the difference between a play and poem? Many actually refer to these as "analysis" skills. But they are unlike any kind of analysis anyone will ever need to do outside of our benighted classrooms.

These programs and reading series are the fruit of an intellectually exhausted literacy industry that lost its way long ago, even as we mutely accepted its misguided agenda—to complicate reading and literacy so that we will purchase its programs and materials.

There is a cost to our somnambulant acceptance of such programs. It means students will never read 15 or 20 books a year, like *Stone Fox* or *Harry Potter* or *The Kite Runner*. It means they will never get around to Elie Wiesel's *Night* or more recent nonfiction books like Susan Campbell-Bartoletti's *Hitler Youth: Growing Up in Hitler's Shadow*. There will be no frequent, extended discussions of these works followed by writing that expresses the two things that matter most when we read fiction or nonfiction:

- What inferences and conclusions can we draw about the people in these books based on their words, behavior, and interaction?
- Do we agree or disagree with the author's message and its implications for our own lives or for the people or culture it describes?

Withal, typical language arts standards rob us of what should be our true priorities: large amounts of meaningful reading, discussion, and writing. Between 50 and 70 percent of class time should be spent in these simple, hugely productive activities. This is especially true for students who need help the most. As Gallagher writes, "struggling readers who do not *read voraciously* will never catch up" (2009, p. 43).

The way we use time in school works against anyone ever becoming a reader, much less a "voracious" one (Allington and others in Schmoker, 2006, Chapter 7). For that to happen, we need to apportion time differently. I like Richard Allington's (2001) guideline: Students should spend a minimum of 60 minutes per day reading, and 40 minutes per day writing.

But right now, we are too busy with the wrong kinds of standards. Partly this stems from misguided—and unnecessary—anxiety about state language arts tests. The best studies, and countries like Finland, point to how counterproductive this is.

The "Terrible Price" of Emphasizing Test Scores

As Gallagher (2009) writes, "a terrible price is paid" when the exigencies of testing supersede authentic literacy activities (p. 26). Teaching to the test, *which so many continue to do,* is both unethical and patently counterproductive.

Multiple studies confirm that teaching to the test in language arts only hurts students. Gay Ivey and Douglas Fisher (2006) found that "no evidence proves that an approach focused on the technical aspects of literacy helps students become more sophisticated in their reading" (p. 17). Others have found that such an emphasis actually impedes a student's ability to meaningfully interact with text or make purposeful connections among ideas (McKeown, Beck, & Blake, 2009).

That's why, in the majority of states, scores have gone up even as National Assessment of Educational Progress (NAEP) scores, a more reliable indicator of authentic literacy, stagnate. As Harold Wenglinsky (2004) points out, high scores on NAEP are the result of asking questions and thinking critically, but only if we use *"real texts—books and stories* rather than short passages" (p. 34, my emphasis). Our focus on language arts standards have backfired; they only succeed in "squeezing out critical thinking skills," and in this way they put "the cognitive development of our students at risk" (2004, p. 35).

But what of the national standards, which are somewhat better than the state standards they replace?

National Standards

Daniel Willingham, the cognitive scientist, has seen the new national reading standards. The problem, he writes, is that "teachers and administrators are likely to read those . . . standards and *try to teach to them*. But reading comprehension is not a 'skill' that can be taught directly" (2009a, p. 1, my emphasis).

That is, we don't learn to read well by being taught reading skills. We learn to read well by reading a lot for meaning: to analyze or support arguments, to arrive at our own opinions as we make inferences or attempt to solve problems. But this is just too boring for our standards writers, whose language betrays the same peculiarly clinical quality. They would have us teaching students to do the following:

- Extract key information efficiently in print and online.
- Apply knowledge and concepts gained through reading to build a more coherent understanding of a subject.
- Draw upon relevant knowledge to enhance comprehension.
- Delineate the main idea (a standard which Hirsch [2009] questions the value of).

These standards are all from national standards documents and written in that grating, fingernails-on-the-chalkboard prose that is unique to such documents. Reading these, I can already imagine teachers drifting away from simple, powerful, team-built reading and writing assignments about authentic texts. I see them drifting toward assignments provided by textbook and basal publishers, toward worksheets and prefab activities and those awful short "books" all "aligned with national standards." There isn't a word here about how much reading students should do (a huge issue that we'll address in a moment).

And that is just the reading standards. There are also the standards for writing, speaking, and listening. They are written to appear as though there are only 10 for each category, but there are actually dozens more embedded within the 10. For instance, for grade 11 and 12 writing standards, I count more than 70 discrete, absurdly over-specified standards in all. Along with reading, there are more than 100 standards to be implemented at one grade level.

How does one organize curriculum around such lists, many of them written in very confusing prose—the "pretentious gibberish" referred to earlier (Garner, 2010)? Confused and overwhelmed by this mass of skills, many schools and teachers will simply resort to programs, worksheets, and workbooks—all "based on national standards!"—that will soon be a ubiquitous feature in our schools. Is this what we wanted when we undertook to create common language arts standards?

Suppose, instead, we had students read, discuss, and write about lots of books, articles, and poems—and that we taught them to annotate and analyze them to make inferences and form their own opinions. Would they really need to be taught to "delineate main ideas," "draw upon relevant knowledge to enhance comprehension," or "form and use the progressive . . . verb aspects"? This is standards-speak—the language of worksheet exercises. Willingham is right: You don't even want to teach such skills, because the best of them are acquired indirectly through lots of exposure to print, close reading, and lots of talking and writing about what you read.

Diane Ravitch (2010) is also right: No state has any business fully adopting these standards until *they have been pilot-tested and refined for a period of years.* No one (myself included) foresaw the unintended consequences of state standards. Let's not now make the same mistake on a national scale. Overall, we need fewer, simpler, more meaningful standards that can't be taught with worksheets.

Before we look at different, simpler, clearer kinds of standards (a somewhat tainted word, I often think), let's look at one country we should emulate if we want all students to achieve both high scores (on any test) and also be authentically literate.

Finland Shows the Way

On international reading exams, Finland achieves the highest scores in the world. It achieves them even though it does not administer such exams to its own students. In fact, like many countries (India, Israel, and others), the Finns do not administer multiple-choice exams at all.

Their success, according to observers, is a result of how much time students spend actually reading during the school day. They found one Finnish student who, upon returning from a year in U.S. schools, had to repeat the entire grade. This is because in the United States, instead of reading and writing, she and her fellow students spent their time preparing for multiple-choice tests or working on "projects" where students were instructed to do things like "glue this to this poster for an hour." Such an activity would never be assigned in Finland, where, by the way, instructional technology has played no role in their success (Gamerman, 2008, p. 2).

It is time for us to consider a new definition of what we call "standards" in language arts. We can change the game by embracing simple, minimalist, commonsense standards like those I'll describe below.

Radically Reconceiving Standards in Language Arts

As we've seen, language arts standards documents tend to be trivial and do very little to clarify *the amount of reading and writing* students must do to become truly literate—which may be the most important "standard" of all. In the main, English language arts standards distract us from the core: ensuring that students can read, write, and talk in ways that prepare them for college, careers, and citizenship.

We have an alternative. I would suggest we take David Conley's (2005) advice and set parameters for the kind and amount of reading, writing, and speaking students would do at each grade level. In addition, we could use something like Conley's four "standards" (as I'm calling them) as the focus for most of the reading, writing, and speaking students do in all subject areas: argument, drawing inferences and conclusions, resolving conflicting views and documents, and problem solving. Again, I find these "standards" attractive because they distill the findings of an excellent study of what college requires (and to a great degree what work and citizenship require). Moreover, *they are simple and clear enough to be memorized and used at every grade level.* And as we saw in Chapter 1, simple, minimal numbers of goals and focus areas are easier to remember and monitor, and therefore much more apt to be implemented.

Conley's standards are also embedded in the new national English language arts standards. I just happen to think that many of the remaining standards are superfluous and distracting. I think great benefits will come from joining only the four college entry standards to Conley's additional recommendation that we should specify

- The number of common books and readings per course,
- The purposes for teaching the common readings, and
- The *number* and *length* of papers we assign, with common scoring criteria.

The best schools I know prove the efficacy of such guidelines. We'll look at some of them in a moment. But I have little faith that we will improve language arts by following a recipe with dozens of arcane, often unnecessary ingredients that doesn't specify how much reading and writing students should do at each grade level.

To see the benefits of a much simpler set of English standards and requirements, let's look at national standards from 1901.

Back to the Future—Again

In a captivating *Education Week* commentary, noted author and former federal education official Diane Ravitch (2010) describes the stunningly simple standards for the old College Entrance Examination for English, developed in 1901. Back then, students were given the titles of 10 substantial books (the list was revised every three years). Students knew they would be asked to write essays about these books, scored with a common rubric; there were no multiple-choice items.

That's it.

As Ravitch points out, these standards had a direct impact on *what* and *how* English teachers taught. Obviously, it meant far more close, analytical reading, frequent practice at persuasive and expository writing, and more writing instruction.

Most of us would make some adjustments to the 1901 exam. But I have to agree with Ravitch that this exam, with its tacit standards (deep reading and analysis; coherent, analytic writing) was, warts and all, *incontestably superior to any test or set of state standards we have produced since.*

Compare the 1901 exam to the pedagogic consequences of our current standards and tests—with items asking students to properly sequence the events in a short reading selection, to select the right "main idea" from a list, and to "distinguish between a major and minor character." None of this is important, and none of it requires a student to *read a single book.* Scores can be artificially pumped up on a diet of 500-word passages and multiple-choice drills (which many students live on).

Or compare the 1901 essay exams to our current graduation tests that ask students to write *without any reference to a text* (which is in direct contrast to almost the only kind of writing they will do in college or careers [Graff & Birkenstein, 2007]). In one state that claims to embrace "21st century learning," the written portion of the graduation exam asks students—I'm not kidding—to describe the view of their city from a hot-air balloon.

We could do so much better. To that end, let's now consider a thought experiment: Suppose that, once students could decode, we decided to use Conley's work as the rough basis for language arts curriculum in the 21st century, from 2nd through 12th grades. What if all reading, writing, and discussion centered on Conley's four intellectual standards? For example, students would resolve conflicting viewpoints as they argued and made inferences about the characters and life issues in *Green Eggs and Ham*, the Ramona Quimby books, Wiesel's *Night*, or current events articles from *TIME for Kids* or *Newsweek*. Importantly, every year, we would have students read at least 20 common and self-selected books, multiple poems, and 30 or more articles or editorials. Students would write approximately one formal essay a month (about their readings), which could be graded with any decent, common scoring guide. (You could actually make a good rubric using *only the best—but not all*—of the criteria found in the national writing standards.) Every week, there would be two or three extended discussions per week about the readings. Finally, let's assume these "standards" are only reasonably well taught, making routine use of the literacy template described in Chapter 3.

Let me add only this—that a school or department leader would meet briefly with each team, each quarter, to review and to discuss progress on common end-of-quarter assessments—in the case of language arts, a text-based essay.

Now ask yourself: If we did these things, but ignored conventional language arts standards, would we be better or worse off? Or more honestly: How many more students would blow the lid off standardized tests *and* be prepared for college and careers?

I can only wish my own daughters had enjoyed such an education.

To ensure, at long last, that students read and write and talk enough to become truly literate—and educated—we need clear, simple standards that sensibly specify how much reading, writing, and speaking they will do—regardless of which teacher they happen to get.

This, too, is simple—and far easier for leaders to monitor for implementation and improvement purposes.

Standards That Count

Our current standards do nothing to protect students from schools that allow a teacher to require students to read only three novels and write three one-page book reports, or no novels and no essays, but 20 poems in "honors" English. (Such was my daughter's experience at schools with very good test scores.)

To avoid this, David Conley recommends that English departments establish a clear agreement for the minimum number of readings and papers to assure common, quality curriculum—an "intellectually coherent program" (2005, pp. 79–82).

All of the following applies fully to 2nd through 12th grade—and some of it to 1st.

Reading

For reading, teams should agree on a specific number of quality "core texts" for every grade level on which students learn to master the core skills of "annotation and close reading." Most of their reading would be in the argumentative/interpretive mode, requiring them to "routinely employ supporting evidence" to "construct their own arguments; agree, disagree . . . critique; and formulate a personal response" to their readings (Conley, 2005, p. 79). Conley would even have English teachers agree on the general purposes or kinds of analysis to be done for some of these "foundational texts" (p. 82). This could be accomplished through common questions or sets of questions developed by the team.

In general, for every English course, I would recommend that teams establish standards that approximate the following, for all students:

- About 15–20 books and plays, depending on length and lexical density
- Multiple poems and short stories (perhaps 5–10 of each)
- 20–40 newspaper/magazine/online articles

These should be divided sensibly among the following categories:

- Fiction (imaginative literature and poetry—about 40–60 percent).
- Nonfiction/literary nonfiction (biographies, memoirs, true stories—about 40–50 percent, of which 25–40 percent can be self-selected).

These readings would be organized by grading period.

Of course, the more time we allot to reading in class, the more reading students can do—and the more they will develop a love of reading. As we've seen, the amounts of reading described above are not unrealistic. Once we reduce or eliminate most of the movies, worksheets, poster making, and test prep activities, we have about 150 hours to play with. Kristie Webster, a 5th grade teacher at J. B. Sutton (with its 100 percent free and reduced-price lunch population) has her students read 35–40 books per year. Over 90 percent of her students pass the state reading exam; 100 percent pass the writing exam.

Again, Allington recommends 60 minutes of reading (and 40 of writing) a day—across the curriculum. If we made this a priority, students could be doing—in all courses combined—at least 150 hours of reading *every year*—enough to work an educational miracle (no matter where a student might begin). This is especially powerful if joined with regular, purposeful discussions about their reading.

Discussion

Discussion is a critical companion to reading. The English curriculum must provide plenty of opportunities for students to share, as Conley (2005) writes, their "personal experiences and values," as well as their opinions and interpretations, as they learn to "support their arguments and provide evidence for their assertions" (p. 81).

I would recommend that students participate in at least three discussions per week about their readings—be they books, poems, or articles. This work would follow the general lines described in the literacy template from Chapter 3. To ensure that these discussions are engaging and successful for every teacher, the team should develop, refine, and share good questions and prompts, informed by something like Conley's four simple standards/habits of mind, starting no later than 2nd grade.

Students will gain immeasurably more from discussions if we make use of a simple rubric like the one described in Chapter 3:

- Always cite the text when making an argument.
- When commenting on or disagreeing with another's conclusions, argument, or solutions, briefly restate what they said, don't interrupt, and be civil and respectful.
- Be concise and stay on point.
- Avoid distracting verbal tics (such as overuse of "like" and "you know").

Conley also recommends that teachers establish clear criteria and ground rules for discussions. Students should learn to avoid overgeneralizations and to distinguish between strong and weak support for their arguments—and to disagree respectfully (2005, p. 82).

To learn these critical life and college-preparation skills, frequent discussion must become a mainstay of literary and textual studies. These two skills—reading and discussion—would in turn be the basis for success on the required writing assignments.

Writing

Schools should establish clear, quantitative agreements about the minimum number of writing assignments all students will complete in the same course. Conley recommends that there be approximate specifications for the number of pages for the agreed-upon papers, including both short and long research papers.

To maintain and achieve good writing "standards" (in the best sense), regardless of teacher, there should be at least one "exemplar" paper for each agreed-upon written assignment. Exemplar papers are exceedingly useful as both teaching and learning tools, as teachers guide students through them before and during the writing process.

Guiding all of this should be a "common scoring guide" with adaptations for specific writing assignments (2005, p. 82). Here, too, and consistent with the findings of the "college knowledge" study, Conley recommends that writing, like reading, have an argumentative focus (p. 81). Students should routinely be asked to write several of their papers in at least two drafts, as the second draft is where we learn the craft of writing (p. 81). As William Zinsser observes, "the essence of writing is rewriting" (in Schmoker, 2006, p. 167).

More specifically, I would recommend several formal papers starting in the 2nd grade: one formal, expository/argumentative paper a month, about nine per year, written in at least two drafts. These should be based on close reading, analysis, and discussion of one or more fiction or nonfiction books, poems, or articles read that month. Some of these papers could be short research papers, with a requirement for a certain number of outside sources.

The papers should be approximately one-and-a-half to three handwritten pages in length in the early grades; they should be three to five typewritten pages in middle and high school (with one longer research paper, as described below).

Importantly, these monthly papers could conceivably constitute the only, or at least the primary, common assessments the team could use to monitor and improve performance in language arts, at any grade level. And remember: An essay is the best possible all-in-one assessment of students' abilities to both read and write effectively. At the end of each month, the team could compare percentages of students who succeeded on common (or highly similar) assignments, with respect to the criteria in their common rubric.

One or two of these assessments could be the basis, each quarter, for the brief data-based conversation the team has with an administrator or teacher leader (as they were with my principal). In English, I can think of no better, simpler way to keep our focus on implementing and improving the most essential elements of literacy and college preparation, at every grade level.

I also believe students should write one long research paper (10–15 typewritten pages) during their senior year (perhaps in conjunction with social studies or science). It would be even better if students wrote shorter research papers at the end of elementary and middle school.

All of this writing should culminate in a presentation. I would recommend students make one or two presentations per semester, from just a few minutes long in the early grades to 10 minutes or longer in the later grades. Some should include the use of Power-Point or other appropriate technology—but as Willingham (2009b) warns, don't let the presentation devolve into an exercise in the features of PowerPoint! During such presentations, all students should be active, taking notes and evaluating the presentations. This is a powerful way to improve one's own speaking and presenting skills.

Presentations should be based on the students' formally written papers. These are the ideal preparation for presentations, promoting both knowledge and confidence. Deep knowledge of a subject—and a well-formulated argument—is one of the best weapons against stage fright.

In all of the above, should there be some amount of independence, occasional exceptions to these measurable specifications? Sure, but only if we continue to use the specifications as a true, agreed-upon reference point.

There will of course be many less formal, single-draft writings and research exercises. These provide students with opportunities to argue, infer, and synthesize about daily readings and discussions "on paper" and to practice the traits of effective writing from their common rubric (such as sentence quality and effective word choice).

Some may be thinking: "Great. But who has the time to grade all these papers?"

Handling the Paper Load

As alluded to in Chapter 3, there are highly effective ways to dramatically increase the amount of writing and writing instruction while *reducing* the amount of time teachers spends grading student papers. We save enormous amounts of time when we teach students to use rubric-based checklists before they hand in their work, when we teach students to do conscientious peer editing (of tremendous value to both writer and editor), and when we use exemplars and carefully teach the elements of our rubrics. We are smart, as assessment expert Rick Stiggins (1994) so often recommends, to evaluate for only one area of our scoring guide at a time. And of course, we must always incorporate those "routine components" of good lessons to which we keep referring: the multiple iterations of modeling, guided practice, and checks for understanding. Doing so ensures higher-quality writing, which is immeasurably easier to score.

We don't have to collect most of the writing students do—only some of it, after our teaching ensures that most of the work will be of good quality. Much of the "grading" we do can be done by walking around the room and scanning or checking off good-faith efforts to use evidence to support arguments and interpretations.

The simple fact is, *students don't learn about the craft of writing primarily from our comments on their papers;* the great majority of what they learn comes from carefully crafted lessons built around exemplars and rubrics (which clarify good writing). For more information and practical tips on reducing the paper load, go to www .mikeschmoker.com. You'll find a document there called "Write More, Grade Less."

Again, feel free to disagree with some of the above details. But I believe such simple, measurable guidelines are vastly superior to current standards. We would be far better off today had we developed and implemented such "standards" at the outset of the reform movement. Our students would be miles ahead in their academic, intellectual, and verbal capacities, and in their powers of thought and expression.

"Power" Standards in English: Three Exemplary Schools

To get a more concrete sense of such standards and how they could operate, let's now look at examples from an elementary classroom, a middle school, and a high school. All of them embody the kinds of "standards" (if that is the right word for them) just described—while virtually ignoring conventional language arts standards. Even so, their test scores are off the charts.

At the Elementary Level

Rafe Esquith is a winner of the National Teacher Award and, according to the *Washington Post,* "the most interesting and influential teacher in the country." He teaches 5th grade at Hobart Elementary, a high-poverty school in the Los Angeles Unified School District.

His English standards consist of clear, consistent expectations for what and how much his students will read and write. Here is a partial list of novels and nonfiction books his 5th graders read and discuss, in school, with Esquith's guidance (Esquith, 2003, pp. 42–43):

Of Mice and Men
The Diary of Anne Frank
Treasure Island
The Adventures of Tom Sawyer
The Adventures of Huckleberry Finn
To Kill a Mockingbird
A Separate Peace
Animal Farm
The Catcher in the Rye
Bury My Heart at Wounded Knee
A Christmas Carol
Great Expectations
Night
The Hobbit
The Autobiography of Malcolm X
Some plays by Shakespeare

That's at least 17 high-quality books or major works; four are nonfiction. Many of these are written miles above what we would assume could be read and understood by 5th graders in such a diverse, high-poverty school. Esquith also teaches and does line-by-line analysis and discussion of multiple other documents with his students, including the Declaration of Independence. And his students read additional self-selected works.

How does he pull this off? By completely ignoring the state standards and the basal reader, which he disdains and refuses to use on principle. "Book publishers," he writes, "don't go to bed at night worrying that Johnny can't read; they worry about sales and profits" (2003, p. 60). He also notes: "I have extra time because the students *never use basal readers. . . .* Have you ever really looked at some of the tasks such materials include?" (2003, p. 43).

I have "really looked" at these tasks, with other educators. After some discussion, it is deeply satisfying to watch it dawn on them that the standards found in these programs directly supplant our effort to prepare students for college. They are the antithesis to the *simple, age-old* methods Esquith employs redundantly: guiding the entire class through each text by alternating between reading out loud to them, discussing and explaining the text where he sees fit, and then having students read independently and interpretively—as he monitors their engagement and understanding. This enables *all* of his students to read and interpret high-quality, challenging books. Esquith knows that telling students to "go home and read this chapter" won't cut it; most won't (2003, p. 40). As in Finland, almost all of this immense amount of reading is done *in class.*

Esquith's writing requirements are equally simple. His students write an essay of the week on what they are reading. That's about 36 essays a year, on argumentative questions or prompts like "Weigh in on George's decision to kill Lennie in Steinbeck's *Of Mice and Men.*" He grades these for spelling, sentence structure, organization, and—emphatically—precision (2007, pp. 51–52).

Esquith knows the unparalleled power of "exemplars" for writing instruction. He regularly types up and distributes certain student essays, with the names removed. "By looking at a range of students' essays," his students "start to see why some are better than others." The result? "Within weeks the kids grow enormously as writers—by constantly writing and evaluating one another's work . . . and they have a good time getting there" (2007, p. 52).

There you have it: a simple curriculum that consists mostly of an established number of the same carefully selected books and other documents, daily discussions of the reading, and about 36 essays, scored and taught using the same clear criteria and exemplars. *And students enjoy this.*

Do such methods put standardized test scores at risk? You decide: Esquith's students score above the 90th percentile; the rest of his school scores in the 40s (2003, p. 60).

At the Middle School Level

At Harlem Village Academies, the focus is on argumentative literacy. As the school's website (www.harlemvillageacademies.org) tells us, "Harlem Village Academies aims for a higher standard: students who think critically [and] argue passionately. . . . It is essential that students become independent and sophisticated thinkers, coherent writers, confident speakers, and avid readers."

Wow. Wouldn't you want your own kid to go to a school that actually lives up to such priorities? Principal Deborah Kenny and her middle school faculty know that literacy is the way up—and that high, clear expectations are everything. The school has been nationally recognized for having among the highest test scores in all of New York City.

Here, too, the reading list is clear and numeric: All 7th graders are required to read 12–14 books; the same 6–8 are required to be read in all classes; another 2–4 come from the "core" or supplemental list; and the remaining 2–4 can be selected by the teacher. These are not suggestions. Teachers must develop a "strong accountability system" to "ensure that all students are *absolutely reading the texts*" (HVA curriculum handout, my emphasis).

In addition, the school has very clear requirements for writing. At each grade level, *every student* writes two multi-draft papers each grading period—a total of eight, about one formal essay a month. For each of these, all teachers use the same three-part rubric (with criteria for ideas, design, and language).

Teachers work closely with each other to implement and improve instruction for this simple, powerful language arts curriculum. As a result of this clear, organized program of reading and writing, students at this Harlem charter school seem to do pretty well:

The percentage of students passing state assessments is typically in the high 90s. Some years, *all* students pass every portion of the test.

At the High School Level

Tempe Preparatory Academy is a grade 7–12 charter school in the Phoenix area. In 9th through 12th grade, English and social studies are combined in a two-hour humanities block. For each grade level, there is

- A clear, generous list of common, required books and readings (including many prominent works of literature, history, and philosophy);
- One formal, two-draft paper per month (nine per year) about the readings; and
- *Daily* Socratic discussions—as much as 90 minutes per day.

In addition, students complete one 15-page paper during the senior year that also serves as the basis for a presentation to a panel of teachers and community members as a graduation requirement.

That's it. That's the curriculum. As we saw earlier, this open enrollment charter school was voted among the best high schools in the Phoenix metropolitan area. The first year of high-stakes testing, it was the only school in the state where 100 percent of students passed *every portion of the test.*

Other than high test scores, what else do these students get for their focus on such a narrow, but powerful, set of standards? This: every one of them—regardless of which teacher they have—will have deeply and daily read, analyzed, discussed, and then written about dozens of common, challenging works of literature, history, and philosophy. They will have written 36 full-blown literary or historical analytical papers and one long, college-level research paper. And they will have completed a presentation based on that paper to members of the faculty and community. Do we really think that our dozens of confusing and irrelevant standards can hold a candle to simple standards like these?

At each of these schools, such simple, minimalist standards ensure a "guaranteed and viable curriculum" of an exceedingly high quality. Any parent or entire community can have total confidence that all graduates—regardless of which teachers they had—will have these common, in-depth experiences that are sure to prepare them for college, careers, and citizenship. And teachers at such schools benefit from a sense of collective purpose few teachers now enjoy.

Simple, Redundant Literacy

Once expectations for reading, writing, discussion, and presenting have been clarified and codified, we should then be sure that our curriculum gives emphatic, ongoing attention to something like the (very unoriginal) literacy template I described in the last chapter. That is, for every assignment that starts with reading, we should

- Teach vocabulary.
- Establish purpose for reading (and hence for talking and writing).
  - *Teach and model* how to annotate/underline/take notes.
  - Discuss the work (using a rubric like the one described above).
  - Write about the work, after reviewing and organizing annotations, underlinings, or notes.
  - Use student and professional exemplars as teaching tools.

I encourage you to revisit the extended version of the template in Chapter 3 (*or your own adaptation of it*) until you have truly mastered these critical elements of literacy instruction. Teams should make its use and implementation a high priority—not only in language arts, as we'll see. It would also be helpful as a resource for mentoring new faculty members and for ensuring clarity and continuity of effective instruction in language arts.

Finally, I would recommend a handy writing resource, now used in hundreds of universities and a growing number of high schools: Graff and Birkenstein's *"They Say, I Say": The Moves That Matter in Persuasive Writing* (2007). This book contains a set of simple templates for setting up argumentative papers and discussions, with exceedingly helpful frames for the essential moves so critical to these activities: how to introduce an argument, how to integrate and explain quotations and supporting material, how to disagree with an author, and how to both agree and disagree— with qualifications. As the authors point out, virtually all writing in academia or the real world is an attempt by writers to present their own thoughts in response to someone else's thoughts—that is, to argue or to address a problem; these arguments employ variations on the same, common templates, phrases, and frames (Graff & Birkenstein, 2007).

• • •

The impact would be *colossal* if, every year, students

• Read, discussed and wrote about 15–20 fiction and nonfiction books (some self selected);
• Read and discussed and wrote about 30–40 interesting poems, newspaper or magazine/online articles; and
• Wrote many short, informal pieces and one longer, formal, argumentative or interpretive paper each month.

An unprecedented proportion of the populace would be educated to a level of sophistication previously unimagined. And our students— regardless of what advantages they did or did not have before they came to us—would be prepared for studies *in every subject area* in ways we've never witnessed.

A Brief Note on Textbooks

Now that we are looking at the content areas, we should revisit the use and importance of textbooks, which we first addressed in Chapter 2. Contrary to current attitudes and practice, textbooks have tremendous value for teaching essential content. And though schools still buy textbooks, many tacitly ignore them or disparage their use. Some barely use them at all, and very few ever teach students how to learn from them.

The educational community was quick to respond to the (legitimate) criticism of textbooks, but quicker still to adopt their horrific replacements: excessive use of lecture, worksheets, movies, poster making, and pointless group work. As a result, Molly Ness observes (as *we* should with some horror) that students have "little direct exposure to print in the content areas" (2007, pp. 229–230). With each passing year, they receive less instruction in how to read non-fiction prose. Mark Bauerlein (2008) similarly laments that students are never taught the kind of careful, analytical "slow reading" that is required in the content areas. In this way, we have infantilized teaching in the content areas.

This has to change. In "Reading for the 21st Century," Michael Kamil writes that academic success depends significantly on students' ability to "comprehend the expository texts in content area textbooks" (in Ness, 2007, p. 229). As we saw in Chapter 3, Louis Gomez and Kimberley Gomez found that amidst all of our distractions, textbooks fall "below the instructional radar in content-area classrooms" (2007, p. 228). This is one of the chief—but still hidden—reasons for poor student performance in the disciplines (p. 225). Gomez and Gomez conclude that K–12 efforts to make text prominent in the content areas "should be redoubled" (p. 228).

Textbooks, along with other carefully selected nonfiction documents, afford students the kind of content-rich, semantically rich prose that students need to both acquire and critically process essential knowledge.

Textbooks: A Two-Year Study

Timothy Shanahan and Cynthia Shanahan (2008) know the value of textbooks—they spent two years studying the ways textbooks were used by historians, scientists, and mathematicians as well as social studies, science, and math teachers. They discovered that textbook reading, though critical to learning in the content areas, was grossly ignored and that students *must be taught how to read textbooks,* at increasing levels of sophistication in all content areas and at every grade level.

There are simple but seldom-clarified "moves" that we must model for students to acquire the essential knowledge in each discipline. These moves aren't complicated. In all the content areas, they require teachers to repeatedly teach and model slow, often methodical kinds of reading for their students—the kind that the teachers themselves do when they read such texts.

The Shanahans found that all such reading is slow and reiterative, but that, in addition, each subject area makes its own specific demands. We'll refer to their subject-specific findings in each of the following chapters.

This is not to forget that other texts are just as important in the content areas—documents of current and historical interest, gleaned from newspapers, "serious" magazines, and the abundance of rich resources available online.

In the following content-specific chapters, we'll see how standards, rightly rendered and organized, can be the foundation for a simple, but rich, college-prep curriculum. We'll see that the core of what and how we teach consists of the same three elements we have been looking at in every chapter: coherent curriculum, effective lessons, and authentic literacy. We'll also refer to the two templates described in Chapter 3.

Social Studies with Reading and Writing at the Core

We are all historians. . . . We are all called on to engage in historical thinking—called on to see human motives in the texts we read.

Sam Wineburg

• • •

Literacy is the key word here, because the teaching of history should have reading and writing at its core. . . . We are aware that we have crafted a decidedly old-fashioned message for a technologically savvy world.

Sam Wineburg and Daisy Martin

• • •

The past is never dead; it's not even past.

William Faulkner

Taught right, social studies and history should be among students' favorite courses. Social studies is the study of *us*—of people and their interactions, both past and present. In social studies, students can make the central intellectual discovery that the past and present interact inseparably and are very interesting on close inspection. Both help us to understand the world and our place in it.

In his autobiography, Norman Podhoretz writes of the epiphany he had in his first year at Columbia University. He realized that history wasn't about "other people"; it was about him—his country, his world, right now. "When I entered Columbia," he writes,

> I thought history was a series of past events. . . . I did not know I was a product of a tradition, that past ages had been inhabited by men like myself, and the things they had done *bore a direct relation to me* and to the world in which I lived. . . . It set my brain on fire. (1967, p. 33, my emphasis)

James Loewen writes similarly of this "direct relation" between historical studies and our immediate lives. History, he notes,

> is about us. Whether one deems our present society wondrous or awful or both, history reveals how we got to this point. *Understanding our past is central to our ability to understand ourselves and the world around us.* (1995, pp. 12–13, my emphasis)

As with literature, social studies and history enlarge us. Both help us understand ourselves; they reveal the hidden or unquestioned cultural and political influences that act on us, often without our consent. Social studies, including large doses of *current* issues and events, allows us to understand those influences. Like literature, social studies broadens our vision and sensibilities beyond the limits of direct experience. In this way, it allows us to have a greater hand in the history we all help to make—in our own nation, town, or temple.

How can ordinary teachers fulfill the promise of social studies with students who seem indifferent to it? There is a way; for social studies to "set the brain on fire," it must have authentic literacy and controversy at its core.

Wisdom, enthusiasm for learning, and college preparation can only come from intensive, frequent reading; talking (*lots* of talking);

writing; and arguing about the people, issues, and events of the past and present. As we've seen, facts are essential. Kevin St. Jarre (2008) speaks for many of us when he writes that students have to know the pertinent facts that precede and inform the issues of our time. But these aren't enough by themselves. He pleads with us to recognize that "what [students] need are more Socratic discussion and reading, more analysis, more writing and *more reasons why they should care*" (2008, p. 650, my emphasis).

If we want students to care about social studies, we must put reading and writing at its core (Wineburg & Martin, 2004).

Social Studies with Language and Literacy at the Core

Literacy is indeed the key to effective social studies instruction (Wineburg & Martin, 2004). Next to language arts, social studies is perhaps the most intensively literate of the disciplines. Both help us understand people and cultures. Both promote the deep understanding of the human condition, which Schlechty (1990) wrote of in his early description of 21st century education. Both require us to read closely and carefully for *nuance*—beyond literal meaning, so that we may be wise, wary consumers of language that is so often used for commercial, political, or self-aggrandizing purposes.

It's all about language. As Stanford's Sam Wineburg writes,

Language is a medium for swaying minds and changing opinions, for rousing passions, or allaying them. This is a crucial understanding for reading the newspaper, for listening to the radio, for evaluating campaign promises, or for making a decision to drink a NutraSweet product based on research conducted by the Searle Company. (2001, p. 83)

Wineburg believes students must be taught to "argue with the text"—both with textbooks *and* other current or historical documents. This makes all students and adults "historians . . . called on to see human motives in the texts we read; called on to mine truth from the quicksand of innuendo, half-truth, and falsehood that seeks to engulf us each day." Social studies is the place to learn this, to "think and reason in sophisticated ways" (2001, p. 83).

Of necessity, we can only learn to "mine truth" from a curriculum rich in opportunities to argue and dismantle written and spoken arguments. Wineburg and his colleague, Daisy Martin, call for an "investigative curriculum" that consists of a "two-part equation . . . the teaching of history should have *reading and writing at its core*" (Wineburg & Martin, 2004, p. 44, my emphasis).

This echoes the sentiments of many prominent history educators. James Banner is the cofounder of the National History Center in Washington, D.C. After studying history teaching in multiple representative states, he and several national experts found that it was deficient in precisely those skills that are "fundamental to historical knowledge and thought: writing well, constructing arguments, reading critically, assessing evidence" (Banner, 2009, p. 24).

It should go without saying that most students won't optimally learn facts (much less care about them) without abundant opportunities to read, write, and talk. As McConachie and colleagues (2006) write, "Students can develop deep conceptual knowledge in a discipline only by using the habits of reading, writing, talking, and thinking which that discipline values and uses" (p. 8, my emphasis).

The benefits of making literacy central to social studies are legion and essential to both the preservation and improvement of culture. As Wineburg and Martin write, "Our democracy's vitality depends on . . . teaching students to be informed readers, writers and thinkers about the past as well as the present" (2004, p. 45).

We don't appreciate deeply enough the outsize value of social studies. If we did, we would do more to preserve its soul: literacy, analysis, and argument. As with language arts, we must rescue social studies from "readicide" and the titanic forces marshaled against literacy, which has been pushed aside in favor of activities that leave students "engaged but illiterate" (Wineburg & Martin, 2004, p. 45).

Skits, Posters, and Social Studies Illiteracy

Wineburg and Martin found that analytic, argumentative reading and writing have been replaced by activities aimed at addressing popular notions about "multiple intelligences or learning styles." To their dismay, they found students performing skits, making posters, and doing an excessive number of PowerPoint presentations (2004, p. 45). More teachers should know that Howard Gardner himself is dismayed by such nonsense in the name of multiple intelligences (Traub, 1998). Such practices supplant our efforts to prepare students for careers and college, ensuring that they will never learn to read deeply and write about social and historical issues—like "defending an argument on why the U.S.S.R. disintegrated" (Wineburg & Martin, 2004, p. 45). We would rather entertain students than teach them.

Wineburg and Martin would instead take us back to the future—to the *old* stuff that ought to inform the *new* core of 21st century social studies.

An "Old-Fashioned" Message

Wineburg and Martin urge a highly unfashionable version of teaching and learning: "We are aware that we have crafted a decidedly old-fashioned message for a technologically savvy world" (2004, p. 44). Social studies educators must break free from fads and embrace what we never implemented in the first place: courses that cultivate students' abilities to participate in "the literate activities that our society demands. This means teaching students to be *informed readers, writers, and thinkers* about the past as well as the present" (p. 45, my emphasis).

Wineburg and Martin recognize that this old-fashioned message is as appropriate now as ever: "The place to teach students to ask questions about truth and evidence *in our digital age* is the history and social studies classroom, and we should not delay" (2004, p. 42, my emphasis).

This emphasis on finding "truth and evidence" in our reading, talking, and writing actually makes social studies simple to teach. It revolves around task, text, and talk. And these are rooted in content—in an organized schedule of essential topics and standards.

Good curriculum should approximate the following:

• Essential topics and standards to be taught, divided by unit and grading period (to ensure roughly common pacing and depth).

• *Selected* textbook pages (*not* the whole book or all of every chapter) aligned with units and topics.

• About 35 (or more) supplementary or primary source documents, including current magazine and news articles, to be read and discussed about once a week. (We'll look at a variety of rich, available resources and opportunities for this at the end of the chapter.)

• Some prepared interactive lectures for each unit to reinforce or supplement the textbook. (See the interactive lecture template on p. 68.)

• Overarching/essential questions for each unit.

• End-of-unit papers or essay question assignments.

• Routine use, for all of the above, of something like the literacy template on p. 74.

That's basically it. Any team of social studies teachers could assemble the topics and textbook pages, the units and questions, and then begin to implement them without much delay. Even a few hours per course can give you enough structure to begin. Of course, once built, refining these standards and their delivery must become the team's active priority: the focus of all professional development, faculty, and team meetings.

We'll start by looking at (always problematic) social studies standards, and then look at how to teach them using the literacy and lecture templates. The last section of this chapter provides an extensive look at the exciting possibilities for supplementary sources—from primary source documents to newspapers, magazines, and online resources.

Overabundant, Poorly Written Standards

* * *

Offered a list of standards, we should scrutinize each one but also ask who came up with them and for what purpose. Is there room for discussion and disagreement?

Alfie Kohn

* * *

In Chapter 4, we saw the damage that can be done by standards documents. To be fair, social studies standards have done less harm than those in language arts. That said, we are wise to have a healthy skepticism for them as well.

Once again, these documents were never field-tested; not a single pilot group of teachers ever tried to *construe, organize, and teach to these,* and then use the findings to refine the initial set of standards. If that process had taken place, every set of state standards would be about half its current size and be vastly clearer and more useful to boot. And there would be a less haphazard connection between these standards and the state exams that purport to assess them (Fuhrman et al., 2009).

As I recommended earlier, start by stripping away most of the verbiage and focus instead on the raw content and topics in the social studies standards documents. After you have selected your essential content standards, replace the verbiage with your own language, questions, and prompts, perhaps reflecting Conley's (2005) habits of mind or the upper end of Bloom's taxonomy. (Remember, if we teach content to Conley's habits or the upper end of Bloom's, the lower end will take care of itself.)

The work always begins with reducing the standards. Once again, I'm looking at a set of standards given the highest rating by a prestigious, nationally known agency. I count 41 topics for the Civil War. That's way too many if we want to teach them in sufficient depth. Take heart in knowing that we have better odds of succeeding on state assessments if we teach far fewer carefully selected standards than if we attempt to teach too many (Ainsworth, 2003a; Marzano, 2003; Reeves, 2003).

The detailed process for reducing the number of standards is found in Chapter 2. In essence, we would have groups of teachers

• Review prescribed standards for a course/grade level, as well as what will be taught above and below their grade level.

• Select their favorite 50 percent of the standards (give or take).

• Use a simple method like dot voting to identify the group's favorite standards—the 50 percent on which the group has highest agreement.

• Prominently post a preliminary set of these "power standards" (Larry Ainsworth's useful term [2003a]).

• Discuss additions, deletions, and modifications.

• Try to come *as close as possible* to the target reduction (50 percent).

• Lay the standards out by grading period and units and determine approximate number of class periods to devote to each, allowing ample time for reading, discussing, and writing.

• *Leave some room* for each teacher to implement some independent assignments.

Once these steps are complete, the document should be finalized (yet always remain subject to adjustment over time) and used as the basis for the team to create all lessons, reading assignments, questions, and writing assignments. Again, it is a good idea to leave about two weeks "free" each semester for individual teachers to pursue their favorite topics or interests (DuFour et al., 2006, p. 65).

Let's now look at how we would work from this initial curriculum map to develop units and overarching questions.

Organizing Around Task, Text, and Talk

Once we have selected and organized our curriculum topics, then what? I find Stephanie McConachie and her colleagues' (2006) simple formula for content area reading very helpful here—their notion of "task, text, and talk." Once we have our curriculum, units, and topics organized by grading period and unit, the authors recommend that we develop two or more questions for each unit. The task is for students to respond in writing to "overarching questions for the unit using evidence from the analysis of primary and secondary sources" (p. 2). Note the emphasis on argument and analysis, recurring themes in the best descriptions of a good education.

Of course, students must be taught, explicitly, how to answer these questions. We must "*apprentice them* into each discipline's way of thinking" (McConachie et al., 2006, p. 2, my emphasis). The term "apprentice" nicely reinforces the elements of good teaching—where the teacher demonstrates analytic reading for the student-apprentice, then observes and offers guidance until the student can do the work independently. These teaching and learning processes are applied to all three parts of the "task, text, and talk" formula.

The "task" in their scheme is akin to the "purpose" for the reading (and talking and writing) in the literacy template. This should include some background on the topic and some attempt to help students to see why the task is interesting (think "anticipatory set").

Let's suppose, for instance, that our elementary or middle school students will be learning about the three branches of state and national government. Their task would be to take notes and summarize the three branches and then argue for why they do or do not think this is an effective way to run a government. (Older students could argue that this system solves or creates certain problems—or both.) The teacher would also provide some background on this topic to pique interest. (Teams should always be sharing both general and topic-specific strategies for creating interest in the common tasks and readings.)

Next, the "text" that supports the task would be, for instance, certain pages from the textbook, selected by the team, describing the branches of government and a newspaper article or primary source document about the separation of powers.

Before having students read either text independently, the teacher would review any potentially difficult vocabulary terms and model critical reading with underlining, annotation, or note taking. Then the teacher would provide guided practice in these processes as students demonstrated their readiness to perform them independently. (We'll look at these steps in detail in a moment.)

The "talk" in the scheme occurs during the modeling and guided practice, as students pair up to discuss and compare their notes and impressions or the teacher decides to call on random students to check for understanding. "Talk" also occurs if, after completing the reading, there is a formal or Socratic discussion. (See the "discussion of text" step of the literacy template in Chapter 3.)

Let's look at one more example in high school world history.

Task, Text, and Talk in World History

Let's suppose that the curriculum topics have been allotted by grading period and that during one of them, the following three units will be taught (as they are in a district I am now working with):

- Renaissance and Reformation
- Encounters and Exchanges
- Age of Revolution

Each unit is about three weeks long. Let's also suppose it is the beginning of the quarter and we will now be teaching the Renaissance. The major topics to be covered are the rise of humanism, prominent Renaissance writers and artists, and conflict between the church and science.

The work would be identical to what we do in the lower grades, as described above. First, the team would develop a task—a question—for the rise of humanism. The task might be: "Write a paper three pages long evaluating the merits and impact of the humanism movement, being sure to cite its origins, key events, and major players. Be sure to share your thoughts and opinions freely, and make connections and comparisons to other historical periods, including our own."

The text could be something like pp. 417–422 of McDougall-Little's *World History,* some samples of art (by da Vinci and Raphael), and writings of the period, including selections from Machiavelli's *The Prince* and Castiglione's *The Courtier.* Students could compare these works to George Washington's "Rules of Civility and Decent Behaviour in Company and Conversation" (circa 1744; available online at www.nationalcenter.org/WashingtonCivility.html). Or ask them to read Froma Harrop's 2010 opinion piece "Slobs and American Civilization," which is about modern manners and the decline of civility. From upper elementary on, students would find these documents readable and fascinating.

The talk in this case comes as pairs and small groups compare and share their notes, underlinings, and perceptions derived from their engagement with the art, readings, and lectures. McConachie and colleagues (2006) recommend that teachers *circulate throughout the discussions,* listening in to gauge students' understanding (p. 11). These would prepare students for whole-class discussions and debates (church vs. science; medieval vs. Greco-Roman values and culture; Machiavelli's cynical-sounding recommendations in *The Prince*—there is plenty of controversy in each).

All of this reading and discussion becomes the basis for the paper the students write—perhaps even short research papers where students simply find and integrate a specified number of sources on their own (like the sources we'll see in the last part of this chapter).

● ● ●

The simple framework just outlined demystifies the organization and delivery of simple, high-quality social studies curriculum. It starts with selecting (only) the most essential standards; dividing the standards by grading period and then into instructional units; coming up with engaging questions or tasks that establish the purpose for the reading, talking, and writing (in line with Conley's [2005] four college-prep criteria); finding suitable texts for these purposeful tasks; and then employing the simple steps in the literacy template for each reading or set of readings. You would supplement this work with interactive lectures using the template in Chapter 3. That's all you need to teach perhaps 60 to 80 percent (or more) of the social studies curriculum.

Any team could implement this simple framework. And students would find such activities far more engaging than typical social studies, which seldom challenges their intellect or includes opportunities for students to discuss and share their thoughts and opinions frequently as they read and learn. As I mentioned earlier, discussion is perhaps students' favorite way to learn (Azzam, 2008).

We can use this framework for any course at any grade level as we prepare record numbers of students for 21st century careers, college, and citizenship. In a moment we'll review in more detail *how to teach* the above—how to incorporate modeling, guided practice, and formative assessment into actual lessons built around the lecture and literacy templates. But first, to demystify this process further, let's look at a few more examples of "tasks" from U.S. and world history, geography, economics, and civics.

Social Studies Tasks: The Student as Expert

Students will enjoy tasks and questions if we encourage them to write and respond to them as experts, with the confidence that comes of having read texts closely, listened, talked, and taken notes. All of these activities prepare students to address, with some authority, questions and tasks like the following:

• Evaluate U.S. behavior during the westward movement, including the War with Mexico, the Louisiana Purchase, and the acquisition of Oregon (argument, inference, drawing conclusions from conflicting views/source documents).

• Give your informed but *personal evaluation and opinions* of Roosevelt's handling of the Depression and the major New Deal programs vs. Harding's handling of the depression of the early 1920s (a *very* interesting comparison).

• Give your informed but *personal evaluation and opinions* of the ethics of walking away from an "upside-down" mortgage. (Lots of pro-con articles on this topic are available online.)

• Give your informed but *personal evaluation and opinions* of life among the ancient Mayans, Aztec, or Incas.

• Give your informed but *personal evaluation and opinions* of which African, Asian, or European country you deem to have the highest quality of life, based on readings and demographic statistics.

• Come up with a realistic post–Civil War Reconstruction program based on your own ideas and a synthesis of the plans you learned about in your textbook and other readings.

• As a public official, defend a system of government—or a combination of systems—with reference to each of the major economic systems: socialism, communism, and democratic capitalism.

• As an expert on a historical period (the Reformation, World War I), write an abbreviated history of that period, with complete freedom to offer your opinions, interpretations, or personal musings about people and events along the way. (This one could be used and repeated liberally, for any unit or historical period at *any* grade level.)

For any of the above, you might add the requirement that students

• Make connections to past or previous periods and events already studied;
• Make connections to current issues, people, or events; and
• Do some independent research to supplement the common readings.

All of the above address Conley's (2005) standards and all rely on readily available or accessible texts—textbooks and supplemental sources that are easy to access online.

But what about all this writing? Does it mean that social studies teachers have to become virtual English teachers? No.

Writing in Social Studies

In social studies, I would love to see students writing end-of-unit papers that are essentially responses to the unit questions—about 10 to 12 short papers per year. These would be based on readings and lectures and would constitute much if not most of the assessment for each unit. Most of the writing should be done in class, in an "open book" environment. This is the kind of truly "educative assessment"—which is itself an educational experience—that we should have embraced years ago (Wiggins, 1998).

In addition, students might further develop one unit paper each grading period or each semester. It would include some independent research (to include a specified number of articles) and would have to meet somewhat higher expectations for length and quality. I'm thinking of these papers as being roughly in the range of two to five pages long, or about 800 words in the earlier years and approaching 2,000 or more as we move toward high school. This amount of writing, done every year, would have life-changing implications for student preparedness for college or careers. And the paper grading load need not be burdensome. Here's why.

As pointed out in Chapter 3, most of the work for these papers would be done in class (with supervision and guidance), in stages, with teacher modeling and checks for understanding occurring multiple times *before students ever hand work in to be graded.* Designated exemplars would be used for every writing assignment, greatly increasing the odds that students will understand and master the essential structure of good papers (which are easier to grade). In addition, students would use the exemplars along with checklists to do their own checks for understanding before ever turning in their papers.

Brief, everyday writings don't always need to be handed in. The teacher can scan them as he or she walks around the room conducting a check for understanding and give credit for adequate completion of the task (for example, for adequately supporting an argument or two with textual evidence).

Again, social studies is not English; English has the primary responsibility for teaching students the finer elements of a writing rubric. In social studies and other subjects, I think it is enough to use a versatile, scaled-back rubric like the following:

• In addressing the question or task, provide a certain number of reasons/citations/direct quotes for each major portion of your argument.

• There must be clear, readable, logical explanations for each citation, linked clearly to the question/argument/learning target.

• You must address major objections to your argument.

If we're smart, we'll teach students not to turn in their papers until they and a peer can attest that they have evaluated it against the exemplar and it meets all the criteria. (For more suggestions on how to increase writing even as we greatly reduce time paper-grading, see the article titled "Write More, Grade Less" on my website.)

As with any assignment, students produce better work (always easier to grade) when we provide full-blown lessons for each phase of the work with modeling, guided practice, and formative assessment.

Let's look more closely at how to do this when we are teaching students to read a text in social studies.

Close Reading in Social Studies

For McConachie and colleagues, the capacity for "genuine historical inquiry" can only be imparted "by *modeling and making explicit* the ways [teachers] want students to argumentatively and analytically read, interpret, and talk about the documentary evidence before them" (2006, p. 12 , my emphasis). This needs to be done continuously. For what it's worth, most educators tell me that we should model how to read, talk, and write "argumentatively and analytically" at least two times per week, every week, at every grade level.

Let's now look at two examples of how a teacher would "model and make explicit" these simple processes for two assignments.

Suppose, in the first case, that we gave 5th or 6th (or 11th!) graders the following task—their purpose for reading the assigned textbook material: "As you read about the Mayans and Aztecs, write an argument for why you would prefer to have been a member of one tribe/group or the other."

The texts would be pages 60–69 (only about six pages total, because of illustrations) from *Adventures in Time and Space*, an upper elementary textbook. (Again, I believe we are smart to have students read no more than half of most textbooks—parts of it slowly and purposefully. That leaves more time to read primary and supplementary source documents.) Start by reading the first paragraph of the section—out loud—as your students read along with you (as you scan the class to ensure engagement). You read that upon entering the city of Tikal 1,800 years ago, the buildings look like a "snow-capped mountain range." You tell students to look at the picture in the textbook of a stunning Mayan temple in Guatemala. Then you read that the city "had a population of 50,000." Stop to "model" your thinking, like so:

> All this is very impressive. That was about AD 200. Such a large city with beautiful architecture tells me they were a very advanced civilization for their time. I will briefly jot this down [which you do, on an overhead projector or Smartboard]. I will look for the answer to this question when I read the next section about the Aztecs.

A few sentences later, after reading some material that is less germane to your task—and you tell them this—you read that the temples were built "to ask their gods for success in battle and for good harvests." You might stop and say something like this:

> This tells me that the Mayan were religious and that they may have been a warlike people. I wonder how warlike, or if they were more or less warlike than the Aztecs? I would have less admiration for a culture that devoted too much of its time and resources to unnecessary wars or wars of conquest.

The intellectual benefits of doing this regularly are invaluable. Make no mistake: this is *how students learn to think.* And it is just as important in high school.

High school students could be given a task like the following: "Evaluate the Progressive Era (1890–1920). Do you agree with, disagree with, or have a mixed opinion of the Progressives' agenda?" (This period is loaded with interesting controversy.)

First, you would give students some background on this very interesting period and compare it to current issues (such as the increasing income gap between rich and poor, homelessness, unemployment, and health care). Then students would read three pages from a textbook like *The American Pageant* (pp. 684–686) as well as one or two online articles. You would do the same kind of modeling we just saw as you read the first few paragraphs about the muckrakers, the Progressive Era journalists. Then you would stop to tell students something like this:

> I like the fact that the muckrakers were looking out for the poor and those without a voice in the early 20th century. I admire that. But it says here that there were "fierce circulation wars" and competition between newspapers during this time. Editors paid a lot of money to writers who could dig deep for "the dirt that the public loved to hate." I'm going to jot that down on my notes [which you would then do, modeling how you usually only jot down brief phrases, not whole sentences]. I'm wondering—are you?—if the money wouldn't cause some of the writers to exaggerate, because their bosses were demanding lots of such stories so their papers would sell. This reminds me of today's tabloids that we see in the checkout line, where the writers are willing to bend the truth because they know it sells. Could some of the muckrakers have done more harm than good? If the textbook doesn't tell me, I may need to seek information from other—maybe online—sources. Now, in the next five minutes, I want all of you to read and annotate/take notes for the next paragraph or two and see what opinions you form or if certain questions occur to you. Then I'll have you pair up and share.

You get the idea. You could conduct the same processes for virtually any reading task that involves note taking, underlining, or annotation. We've seen the value of textbook reading in earlier chapters. But you could also model and provide instruction for how to read current articles, opinion pieces, primary historical documents, or demographic tables on various countries, states, or cities. We'll discuss their promising possibilities in a moment.

When we routinely "model and make explicit" how we as adults read, think, and make connections, students learn to do it too. Furthermore, they will see that such close, insightful reading *is within their reach*—that all of them can do such reading and thinking, which is central to an education.

Let's look now at how the remaining elements of good instruction are employed in this simple read, talk, and write template.

Checking for Understanding

Modeling, however invaluable, is never enough. We have to follow through with the other routine components of good lessons—guided practice and checks for understanding. For example, after you model your thinking for the Mayan/Aztec assignment, you would let students read the next two paragraphs alone while you circulate and observe (guided practice). Look for patterns of strength or weakness: Are students recording important information (like the fact that one of the tribes had mastered very sophisticated farming methods)? Do they know how to abbreviate their notes and annotations to save time—but in a way that they can make sense of later? Do they need more modeling right now? Or are they ready to "pair up" and share what they have underlined or written in their notes? After they pair up, you can call on pairs of students randomly to see how well they can explain the connection between their notes and the demands of the task (to argue their preference to have lived as a member of one tribe or the other). They may need more help and modeling in how to make and record these connections—followed by more guided practice and formative assessment.

At the right point, you would let students finish the document independently and then write their informal papers. This, too, would be taught and modeled, working from an exemplar of such writing (see the literacy template in Chapter 3). It could be graded quickly for logic and content using a rubric like the one above—or possibly by just walking around. Thus is a worthy education acquired—the result of using variations on the same simple template frequently and redundantly.

By design, this template shares the same elements as those of effective interactive lectures, which we'll look at now.

Interactive Lectures in Social Studies

As noted in Chapter 3, lecture, done right, is a "marvel of efficiency" (Silver et al., 2007). It allows us to impart copious amounts of content knowledge in the subject areas and productively supplement what is lacking in the textbook. But, as we saw, lecture too often devolves into "a waste of precious classroom time" (2007, p. 26).

To be effective, interactive lecture must also incorporate the routine components of good lessons so often referred to in these pages. Here, too, I recommend that you visit the more detailed and very helpful summary of interactive lecture found on p. 68.

In essence, effective interactive lecture in social studies requires that we do the following:

• Begin the lecture by providing essential or provocative background knowledge and a task, usually in the form of a question students will respond to.
• Ensure that the lecture stays closely focused on the task.

- Ensure, through guided practice and formative assessment, that students are on task and learning; do this by circulating, observing, and listening as students take notes and pair up to process each chunk.
- Avoid talking for more than five to seven minutes without giving students an opportunity to connect learning to the essential question or task—to review their notes and pair up to compare their connections and perceptions with others.
- Ensure, in discussions, that all students respond multiple times during the lecture (Marzano, 2009).
- Reteach or clarify whenever a check for understanding indicates that students have not mastered the material in the previous chunk of the lecture—and only move on when we feel they are ready.

Such a template, like the literacy template, could be used frequently and liberally, having a positive impact on a generous portion of the curriculum. In combination, the majority of instruction in social studies could be built around these two templates.

Again, the use of these simple strategies is contingent on our commitment to a severely reduced, viable diet of standards and topics, which creates time for students to digest, discuss, and write about what they are learning, to discern historical patterns, and to make connections between past and present (Marzano, 2003).

And, once again, *none of the above must be done perfectly* to have an immense and immediate impact. Social studies education will be vastly more interesting for students the moment we adopt these simple activities so rich in content, literacy, *and verbal interaction.*

Perhaps the most promising development in social studies is the effort to more routinely incorporate documents that supplement—and often undermine (as they should)—the textbook: primary source documents, newspapers, magazines, and articles, all of which are so readily available online. All of these documents would be taught using the same simple literacy template found in Chapter 3.

Primary Sources and Current Events

I honestly believe that social studies could be on the cusp of its greatest moment—that it could soon be a subject students come to love and look forward to. But to ensure that happens, we must infuse generous amounts of current and historical texts into students' weekly social studies diet. Such documents should include primary source documents, alternative histories, and also current issues and events found in newspaper and magazine articles. These should be introduced no later than the upper elementary grades.

Such supplemental texts could be a real game-changer, with a profound impact on students' sense of what history is and how it connects to their personal lives, culture, and communities. For all the value of the textbook as a conventional overview of history, students need plenty of opportunities to read and argue about what they find in a variety of source documents, past and present. Such an education is both personally and intellectually empowering and would accelerate their education by several years. I believe it could have a marked impact on general maturity levels.

There's a real breakthrough awaiting us here. To make these good things happen, teams of teachers must become avid, systematic collectors of documents (and good, field-tested questions). Many should be tied to instructional units, but any good or timely document will provoke curiosity and interest in the world. Some of these texts and questions should be shared within the school, district, region, and even state.

All we need are good texts that give students a chance to ask or discuss versatile questions like the following, which could be endlessly adapted:

- Do you agree/disagree with the author?
- What inferences, interpretations, or connections can you make using the text?
- Do you approve or disapprove of this past or present policy, person, or movement? What lessons can we learn from it/them?
- What problem(s) does the study of this person or policy help us solve?
- What can we infer from this text about this particular time, place, or culture?

I have seen what happens when students have the chance to closely read, talk, and write about historical documents and current articles, how it stirs their curiosity or outrage, their sense of fairness as they see how the world works—and how to make it better. We have to stop indulging in the fantasy that students don't care about ethics, human rights, war, climate change, global trade, and the best and worst of popular culture. They care—greatly—if given the opportunity to tackle a good text, knowing they will have a chance to talk, listen, and respond to others.

Write on the Text!

Any true education must include something woefully lacking in the majority of classrooms: regular opportunities to mark up, annotate, or highlight one- to three-page articles and documents. Writing *on the text itself* is a primary, essential intellectual experience—and it is mystifyingly rare in K–12 schools. (My daughters each had *one teacher* who took close reading and annotating seriously.) Students can't do this with textbooks. But we need to teach them, ceaselessly and at ever-higher levels of sophistication, how to annotate and underline and form arguments from their reading.

To those who say there isn't time, I can only say: Yes, there is. If there doesn't seem to be, then we are trying to teach too many standards—or we are relying excessively on worksheets, movies, or ill-conceived projects. There is time to read and discuss current and primary source documents every week or two at the very least— enough to transform social studies education.

I have divided the following supplementary documents into my own somewhat arbitrary categories—and only as suggestions. The categories overlap. I will try to explain the function of each category and how it fits into the overall scope of social studies and history courses.

Historical and Primary Source Documents

About once a week, at most grade levels, students should have the chance to read from eyewitness or contemporary accounts, or from official or notable documents from the historical periods they are studying. Only this can give them an up-close, unfiltered sense of what people thought and did at the time the pieces were written. This deepens our understanding of people and institutions of the past in a way that no textbook, by itself, can do.

For instance, every student should have the chance to read General Sherman's letter to the mayor and council of Atlanta— sometimes titled "War Is Hell." In it, Sherman forcefully explains the reasons for his scorched-earth tactics. There is no better way to get into the mind of a 19th century warrior, or to evaluate the logic of the argument for total war that applies to Sherman's time as well as ours.

When studying the early explorers, students can read selections from Columbus's personal diary, which is written in clear, concrete language (4th or 5th graders could read it). These provide us with excellent opportunities to make inferences and draw conclusions about Columbus himself as well as the late 15th century European mind-set. Students could defend or debate those values against our own, or against the backdrop of his era. Or we might have them analyze the conflict between the sometimes damning contents of the diary and Dimitri Vassilaros's (2008) article, "Columbus Was a Hero."

When students are studying the rise of industrial America, they could read an excerpt of Harriet Hanson Robinson's account of life as a mill worker in Lowell, Massachusetts, where even 10-year-old girls worked *14-hour days*. (A two-page excerpt of Robinson's text can be found, along with many other fascinating historical documents, at Fordham University's Internet Modern History Sourcebook, available online at www.fordham.edu/halsall/mod/modsbook.html.) A good question for this and similar texts: What differences and similarities do you see, between then and now, in our attitudes toward women and girls—or people in general?

Lincoln's second inaugural address abounds in rich implications about just war and the case for the Northern cause. We could have students write an argument against the address and its message, from the perspective of a Confederate official.

The Analects of Confucius make very interesting reading: Confucius's simple aphorisms had a profound, enduring impact on China's history, culture, and development. *They could be read by most 3rd or 4th graders.* There is no way to understand their rich appeal without reading a few of these eloquent teachings, available online at http://eawc.evansville.edu/anthology/analects.htm. Students can argue about their merits and compare Confucius's perspective to current or less ancient notions of wisdom.

There are limitless opportunities to match such documents to periods we are studying, which would deepen understanding of human nature and enhance students' global perspective and understanding. Some examples for U.S. history follow:

• President Jackson's message to Congress "On Indian Removal" (1830), which led to the Trail of Tears. No textbook summary can capture the mind-set of Jackson's era like a one- or two-page selection from this address to Congress.

• Selections from President Reagan's "Tear Down This Wall" speech.
• Martin Luther King Jr.'s "Letter from a Birmingham Jail."
• Supreme Court decisions: These primary source documents are rich in history and can be taught if we provide some background, vocabulary, and guidance to optimize student understanding. I had great luck teaching *Plessey v. Ferguson* to 7th graders.

Primary source documents are an obvious, critical supplement to textbook reading, but there are other secondary source documents that would greatly enhance social studies: short biographies and excerpts from alternative histories, current events articles, and other accessible sources.

Short Online Biographies

These readable, one- or two-page documents give us a deeper look than the textbook provides. For each, we could have students carefully read and annotate short online biographies as they answer questions like, "What do we learn from this person's life about their time and place and/or our own lives, time, or current issues?"

Clara Barton, John Brown, Genghis Khan, Akbar the Great of India, Helen Keller, and Aristotle are fascinating people, but only if we carefully teach, model, and apprentice our students into how to read brief biographies for the implications and connections they have for their time and ours. Reading about, writing about, and discussing such figures would be highly engaging for students.

Alternative Histories

There is a rich variety of alternative views of history, in short or long forms:

• Thomas E. Woods Jr.'s writings about the Great Depression would be fascinating to high school students—particularly the first few pages, in which he compares the depressions of the 1920s and the 1930s with our more recent "Great Recession" (see online at www.campaignforliberty.com/article.php?view=275).

• James W. Loewen's book, *Lies My Teacher Told Me,* is packed with provocative interpretations of U.S. history (1995). Or go online to see his fascinating study of Helen Keller, whose ardent adherence to communism is seldom contained in traditional history books (see www.ibiblio.org/pub/electronic-publications/stay-free/archives/18/loewen.html).

• Michael Medved's books and online articles offer very well-written views on cultural issues from a right-leaning perspective.

• From the left, Howard Zinn's famous *A People's History of America* (2003) has now been published in a form appropriate for elementary and middle school (with Rebecca Stefoff, 2007/2009).

Here I must pause to suggest how books like Zinn's or Medved's would make it simple to teach U.S. history effectively, from 3rd grade up, and would address the perennial controversies over which standards to teach and which viewpoints should predominate. Many people rightly note, for instance, that conventional textbooks tend to avoid controversial information and perspectives in our history. Why not have students read Loewen's book or Howard Zinn's *A People's History of the United States* (or its elementary-grades version) alongside the textbook—or either of these books alongside the conservative *A Patriot's History of the United States* by Larry Schweikart and Michael Patrick Allen (2004; an elementary version is now being written of it as well)? All of these books would provoke lively discussions.

Even if our curriculum focused mostly on close analysis and discussion and writing about the treatment of U.S. history in (1) textbooks and (2) two conflicting texts like Zinn's or Medved's, the experience would be transformative. Though Zinn's book can be found in many high schools, I seldom find that its contents and arguments (like our textbooks) are read carefully, analyzed, debated, or written about.

Current Events and Late-Breaking News

Reading about and discussing current events and late-breaking news would be very exciting for students. We need to consider making such assignments a weekly routine.

Not long ago, Haiti's earthquake and recovery effort was the big story. Students should have had a chance to read articles like the one I read this morning, explaining why some Haitians have mixed feelings about the U.S. military even as it provides needed aid to their troubled country. This is the "hook" that makes it possible to discuss U.S. involvement in third world countries over the centuries. Many Haitians resent this involvement, which they believe has had negative long-term effects on their development.

History, as we know, is always repeating itself—*with differences.* Students need to develop a sense of such patterns and differences; they will soon enough be our voting citizenry, and their views on military matters will be shaped mightily by what they know about past and present military involvements. The same goes for domestic issues like health care, where to cut state budgets, or how to regulate Wall Street banks without harming them or our long-term economic health.

All of these issues would enliven social studies and can be easily shown to connect richly to the past. They are tomorrow's history— just as the current health care debate can only be understood if you know something about the 1994 attempt to launch a national health care system (overseen by our current secretary of state, Hillary Clinton).

There is so much opportunity here for analysis and discussion: elections, people in the news (Harry Reid, Sarah Palin)—these are the "hooks" for enjoining students in the kind of reading, annotating, discussing, and writing that students need to prepare for the world they are entering.

And this doesn't only apply to middle and high school students. TIME for Kids and similar publications feature current events written at 2nd and 3rd grade reading levels. I'm looking at one such article about the reasons for the plummeting population of tigers in the world and the implications this has for their ecosystems. It contains statistics, information on efforts to save the tigers, and interviews with scientists. Great stuff. Other articles include "Reaching Out to Haiti" with information about comparative earthquake magnitudes, population, and poverty rates. "The State of America's Kids" has graphs and statistics about health (like child obesity trends). "A Shift in the Senate" is about the balance of power, historical perspective, and the impact of a Senate shift on current legislation. And all of these articles are full of what is increasingly important to the social studies: percentages and statistics, many of them featured graphically in charts and tables. All of these articles are written in 2nd and 3rd grade language. Is there any defensible reason not to make such documents a staple of instruction in social studies?

Again, I offer an important caution: *Please ignore the ever-present questions, activities, and worksheets that accompany such materials— they are seldom worth your time. Instead, simply have students read carefully to argue, infer, and make their own connections and conclusions as they read.*

Resources for Ongoing Issues, Controversies, and Culture

In this category, we find writings on more enduring if somewhat less timely issues:

• Allan Bloom on rock music; you can't miss with excerpts from *The Closing of the American Mind* (1988). Or read Stanley Kurtz's 2007 article on Bloom and rock and roll, "*Closing,* Still Open," in which Mick Jagger denigrates rock music. I *guarantee* an interesting discussion.

- The *New York Times*'s Nicolas Kristoff (2009) on microloans. "Sparking a Savings Revolution" is a simply written article about the outsize economic impact of helping third-world citizens to set up even small bank accounts.
- "Best. Decade. Ever." by Charles Kenny (2010). This fascinating *Foreign Policy* article argues that the first 10 years of the 21st century were humanity's finest—even for the world's bottom billion. It is a provocative and highly readable piece.
- "The Pros and Cons of Globalization," *BusinessWeek* (2000).
- "Mass Transit Hysteria" (2005) by P. J. O'Rourke has compelling stats arguing *against* the expansion of mass transit.

Of course, any of the above can be matched with an opposing view and debated. To that end, the website ProCon.org is a cornucopia of information on both sides of numerous enduring issues (more on this in the science chapter). FactCheck.org is an excellent source for resolving conflicting views and source documents on a variety of current and ongoing issues. For innumerable issues, it shows how both sides distort facts for political reasons. Indexmundi.com has a variety of demographic and quality of life statistics for nations, states, and cities. These sites offer rich opportunities for students to compare and evaluate the not-so-visible factors that affect people's lives.

On video, I love shows like *Fareed Zakaria GPS* on CNN, or ABCs *This Week*—especially the roundtable. Short, occasional clips would stimulate discussion and provide good models of clear, logical expression. If not overused, these can be a rich resource.

Lastly, students' own historical writings can be a fascinating resource for other students. We should collect good examples of student papers that are worthy of our analysis and discussion. Since 1987, Will Fitzhugh's quarterly *The Concord Review* has published the best examples of high school historical writing (any writing!) you'll find anywhere. Get a subscription to *Concord Review* at www.tcr.org.

There is nothing entirely new here. What *is* new is the emphasis teams would give such documents: to searching for them and then making them a much higher priority in social studies. All we would need is maybe one good text per week—about 35 documents in all. Course-alike teams could do much of the up-front work during scheduled team times or be paid to do this in the summer. It would be well worth it. Even one weekly experience would assure that students had abundant opportunities to practice deep, line-by-line reading and annotation. It would enliven students' interest in both the present and the past and reveal their seamless connections.

Add it up: This alone, done about once a week for 10 years, would lead to students having discussed and written about 300 such articles or documents by the time they leave high school.

A Whole New World

• • •

Social studies is the study of the world.

Teacher Eugene Simonet (played by Kevin Spacey) in *Pay It Forward*

• • •

Let's take stock. If students read, wrote, and talked as I suggest they do in this chapter—and if they closely read, argued, and wrote about the issues they encountered in textbooks, primary source documents, newspapers, magazines, and online articles every year—the cumulative benefits would be unparalleled. Average students in the United States would be more intellectually attuned, informed, articulate, and ready to make their way in the world than any previous generation.

We can make this happen. Right now.

Let me end by sharing two brief stories that convince me of this. Not long ago, I was teaching in a middle school history class. I decided to have students read the majority opinion in *Plessey v.*

Ferguson, in which Justice Henry Billings Brown writes his reasons for believing we should not allow people of color on the same trains as white people. Here we have a bright, educated man explaining, on behalf of several other highly educated men, why we should separate the races on trains and in public places in general.

After reviewing some vocabulary, sharing some background, and *modeling my own reading of the first couple of paragraphs,* I had the students closely read a selected portion of the text. As they read, I walked around to make sure they were on task and to see how well they were doing. After a few such iterations of reading, pairing, sharing, and modeling, they read the rest of the document on their own. Then we had a very productive, stimulating discussion; every student participated. In the heat of all this controversy, I had them write their arguments, which they did eagerly, as I walked around monitoring their efforts.

I did nothing exceptional—nothing any teacher couldn't do. But when the class was over, *the students clapped.* Not (believe me) because of anything I did, but because students really do enjoy these kinds of activities.

A while later I was in a high school leading a similar discussion about a controversial document with 11th graders in a U.S. history class. Again, every student seemed to deeply enjoy the opportunity to read slowly, underline, annotate, share thoughts in pairs, and then discuss the issues as a class. Everyone participated—eagerly. I later found out that most of them *had never done anything like this before.*

We are sitting on a real opportunity here. And the same opportunity awaits us in science.

Redefining Inquiry in Science

Inquiry science occurs when students use reading, writing, and oral language to address questions about science content.

Susanna Hapgood and Annemarie Sullivan Palincsar

• • •

Hands-on . . . activities may have overshadowed the importance of developing science content ideas.

Kathleen Roth and Helen Garnier

Like English and social studies, science curriculum is in need of significant revision, based on what I believe is an emerging consensus: that science, too, is best learned through an emphasis on content presented through intellectually engaging, age-old literacy practices. If we combine these with the right kind (and the proper amount) of hands-on labs and activities, then high-quality, effective, engaging science instruction will be within any teacher's reach.

The simple, essential ingredients for the majority of effective science curriculums are

- Close reading of selected portions of science textbooks;
- Regular reading and discussion of current science articles;
- Interactive lecture;
- Writing—from short, almost daily pieces to longer, more formal pieces; and

• A reasonable number of carefully designed science labs and experiments that reinforce the content being learned.

In this chapter we'll see—against the conventional wisdom—that an overemphasis on activities may be interfering with what matters most in science learning: opportunities for repeated reading, discussion, and writing about essential science content. These are finally being acknowledged as the core of authentic, *inquiry-based* science and are vital to critical thinking and reasoning in the sciences. And as with English and social studies, we'll see how science-related newspaper, magazine, and online sources could add an exciting element to science education.

Task, Text, and Talk in Science

As with language arts and social studies, effective science instruction consists of simple, effective combinations of purposeful reading, talking, and writing—of "task, text, and talk" (McConachie et al., 2006). To learn at advanced levels, students need frequent opportunities—every week—to carefully read science-related texts and to perform oral and written tasks within the framework of a coherent body of science content. They need these opportunities at every grade level.

This is why a growing number of prominent science educators are urging us to reevaluate our current priorities. They aren't telling us to abandon labs and experiments. But they *are* asking us to reexamine the assumption that we need *more* hands-on science labs or that such activities are the essence of science education.

The benefits of such a reversal would be considerable. Kathleen Roth and Helen Garnier are senior research scientists at the Lesson-Lab Institute in California. They found that the highest-achieving countries had one crucial element in common: their "science lessons focused on content," on "engaging students with core science ideas." Not so in the United States, where content is pushed aside in favor of "engaging students in a *variety of activities*" (2006–2007, p. 16, my emphasis). Worse yet, the majority of these activities have little or no connection to essential science content.

Throughout these pages, we've heard from cognitive scientists that critical thinking and content knowledge are interdependent and are best learned simultaneously (Hirsch, 2008; Willingham, 2009b). Science educators concur. In "Characterizing Curriculum Coherence," Roseman, Linn, and Koppal stress that for students to make all-important connections between the life and physical sciences, they must acquire a coherent, "central core" of science content (2008, p. 17). Science professor and author James Trefil has no patience with those who believe we can scant science content and expect students to learn the science they need. "In the end," he writes,

> you cannot think critically about nothing—the concepts you manipulate have to be in your mental arsenal before you can begin manipulating them. . . . There is no point teaching students to think critically about global warming if they don't know the basics of planetary energy balance. (2008, pp. 176–177)

This doesn't mean we need to know everything about an issue before we can think critically about it; indeed, we learn content best by evaluating and analyzing its meaning *as we learn* (Silva, 2008; Willingham, 2009b). Even so, if we don't know the essential science concepts that inform an issue, then we are at the mercy, in any argument, of those who do.

But here, too, less is more; we must keep our focus on essential science concepts, learned deeply.

Less Is More: Fewer Science Standards

In the highest-achieving countries, the number of core concepts and standards taught in science is less than half that of the United States. The Australians and Japanese know that in-depth learning is impossible with a set of standards that foolishly "goes beyond" the essential ideas needed at each grade level to understand science (Roth & Garnier, 2006–2007, p. 24). Nonetheless, curriculum experts Rodger Bybee and Pamela Van Scotter observe that here in the United States, science curriculum routinely "suffers from a lack of focus; teachers are expected to cover too many topics" (2006–2007, p. 45). Gerald Wheeler, the executive director of the National Science Teachers Association, writes that our standards documents contain "far too many concepts to address" (Wheeler, 2006–2007, p. 31).

This is not news. But we have yet to fully, publicly own up to the disastrous effects of our overlong standards documents: "curricular chaos," which results when teachers realize they can't teach to all the standards, so each teaches to his or her personal favorites. Despite wide acknowledgment of this phenomenon, entirely different standards continue to be taught in the same course (Berliner, 1984; Marzano, 2003; Schmidt, 2008).

The higher-achieving countries make sure this doesn't happen. They focus less on activities, and more on *actually teaching* a much smaller set of essential content standards in sufficient depth to be meaningful and engaging for students. As we'll see, literacy is central to their success in both mastering science and learning to think critically about it.

What, then, about the role of hands-on science activities, labs, and experiments? These findings may surprise some of you.

The Trouble with Hands-On Science

As we saw earlier, U.S. science instruction is typically built around a variety of activities that often have little or no connection to essential science content (Roth & Garnier, 2006–2007).

My daughter took an advanced high school science course from a teacher who proudly proclaimed that no textbook would be used in the course—it would consist entirely of hands-on activities. Now in college, she is grateful for the teacher who *did* have his students read liberal amounts of complex, content-rich textbook material. This prepared her to understand the challenging textbooks she now reads routinely in her university courses. Interestingly, my daughter continues to disparage the activities she has to complete in her college science labs, where students do lots of measuring, pouring, and filling in of blanks—but not much learning.

Is this unusual?

Science educators are confirming, in force, that much hands-on lab work often has very limited value. Somewhat perversely, these often supplant the mastery of essential content, which is learned largely through interaction with text, effective lectures, and discussion.

In his interviews with students and teachers, James Trefil found that most "labs" are carried out pro forma. Students typically "game" the activity by merely working backward from the correct results, learning nothing in the process. He believes there are "elements of faddishness in the current excitement" about labs and hands-on activities, which are usually "an unnecessary frill" (2008, pp. 188–189).

Bruce Alberts, the former president of the National Academy of Sciences, does not disagree. As a student, he found science content fascinating but loathed the typically "tedious cookbook . . . boring laboratory exercises." It was only when he was given the freedom to devote himself to reading and absorbing the content of the discipline that he "discovered the excitement of science" (2006–2007, p. 18).

More Literacy, Fewer Labs

Alberts's experience echoes what Timothy Shanahan and Cynthia Shanahan found in their two-year study on the value and use of textbooks. Scientists told the researchers that the true "essence" of the scientific disciplines was learned not as much from labs as from the slow, close reading of *science textbooks* (2008, p. 54).

The countries with the highest science achievement not only devote *less* time to hands-on activities, they also make sure that their labs connect directly to the content being taught. In the United States, however, science activities did not typically support a coherent body of essential science concepts. Most science activities in U.S. classrooms "contained no explicit science content at all" (Roth & Garnier, 2006–2007, p. 20)—and according to the National Research Council, most high school science labs were "poorly integrated into the rest of the curriculum" (Bybee & Van Scotter, 2006–2007, p. 44).

There you have it. Good science labs, richly connected to science content, are essential. But prominent science educators are calling us to put the brakes on the popular notion that science is optimally learned through activities. This is a myth. It is time to reevaluate the profusion of disconnected, ill-conceived, "cookbook laboratory exercises" (Wenglinsky & Silverstein, 2006–2007, p. 25). They add little value to science learning and emphasize only "procedures rather than learning goals" (Perkins-Gough, 2006–2007, p. 93).

These are the "brutal facts" of science education in the United States. Surely we can do better. We can arrange for all students to learn the same essential content, using the same procedures for selecting, organizing, and teaching that content described in Chapters 2 and 3.

Then, once the content is selected and organized, we must resist the knee-jerk imperatives of multiple-choice teaching and testing. The best way for students to learn is not by having them memorize disconnected facts. It is by providing frequent, focused opportunities for close critical reading, talking, and writing about science concepts.

Effective Science Inquiry—Through *Literacy*

As we've seen, there is a growing acknowledgment that reading (including textbook reading), writing, and talking are essential features of a quality education in any discipline—including and notably in science. As Louis Gomez and Kimberly Gomez argue, we are in need of "an intensive reading in science infusion" (2007, p. 225). A recent report from the National Research Council supports these findings:

> Being science literate entails being able to read and understand a variety of science texts to form valid conclusions and participate in meaningful conversations [discussion] about science. (In Zmach et al., 2006–2007, p. 62)

One of the report's key recommendations was for teachers to ensure that they "engage students in extensive reading of content area texts" (in Zmach et al., 2006/2007, p. 63). We saw how the scientists in the Shanahan and Shanahan study noted that the very "essence" of science was learned from close, careful reading of science textbooks. Literacy is also the basis for "inquiry"—critical thinking—in science.

In "Where Literacy and Science Intersect," Susanna Hapgood and Annemarie Sullivan Palincsar make clear that true science *inquiry* occurs when students engage in "reading, writing and oral language to address questions about science content." This is precisely how students learn "to build their capacity to engage in scientific reasoning . . . how to generate claims [arguments] about a phenomena" (2006–2007, p. 56). Their article affirms the need to make the textbook central—and also to teach and model how to read, write, and discuss science content as we learn it.

One of the best science lessons I ever observed was an expressly Socratic discussion in a high school chemistry class. The day before, students had learned the molecular explanation for why water changes forms under different conditions. First, the teacher had students arrange their desks into a circle—so that the discussion would be face to face. (Try this; you'll be surprised at how much richer the interaction will be.) Then they were asked leading questions about such phenomena as condensation, fog, and evaporation ("What do you think happens if . . . ?"). As the students discussed, the teacher would occasionally nod or comment briefly to indicate that they were on or off the right track. Students listened to each other intently and worked hard to articulate their thoughts as they questioned and corrected each other, always building on or responding to each other's remarks—or the teacher's cues.

For a full hour, these students were expanding both their mastery of these concepts and their powers of listening, thought, and expression. They were doing this in the only way possible—through language, the medium of thought. Students clearly enjoyed the discussion. All students participated, and several kept discussing the topic after the bell rang (reinforcing, once again, Azzam's finding that 83 percent of students find discussion their *favorite way to learn* [2008]).

Now multiply this experience by about 50 (which is about how many such discussions occur in that chemistry class each year), then add writing, and what do you have? A phenomenal chemistry education—simply achieved.

Language, Not Labs

Language is the medium of thought and its refinement. Inquiry-based reading, writing, and discussion—not cookbook science labs—are the essence of true inquiry-based science. That means we must literally teach students, starting in the early grades, to read science texts as we "consistently model how to read critically and question ideas presented in the text," according to Hapgood and Palincsar. Moreover, they found that "students who used textbooks" and wrote purposefully about the content "learned the most content" (Hapgood & Palincsar, 2006–2007, pp. 57–58).

But we can't just assign textbook chapters. That won't work. We need to vigorously implement the same simple elements of instruction we've been looking at. Courtney Zmach and her colleagues implore us to teach students *how* to read, talk, and write purposefully about science texts with lessons replete with "think-pair-share, paraphrasing[,] . . . modeling, guided practice and chances to apply the [reading] strategy independently"—the same "routine components" Marzano recommends for all lessons (Zmach et al., 2006–2007, p. 63). Strategic reading, talking, and writing (when will we learn this?) are perhaps the truest forms of "active learning."

And once again, *students will enjoy this.* Hapgood and Palincsar found that students are "eager to talk, read, and write" about what they learn in science. They love to "compare their thinking with others' thinking, actively communicate with one another and express their ideas through words and graphics" (2006–2007, p. 56).

Zmach and her colleagues made the same discovery: students were "eager and engaged" during their reading in science lessons. They found that the readings themselves "stimulate lively discussion." I always had great luck with reading, discussion, and writing activities when I actively taught these processes like I would any good lesson—with modeling, guided practice, checks for understanding, and adjustment.

What can we expect if we turn the ship of science instruction in this radically new direction toward literacy practices (and joined to the most basic and effective teaching practices)? Great things, indeed: "significantly higher" scores on both reading and science tests, more positive student attitudes toward science, and "more confidence in their capacity to learn science" (Hapgood & Palincsar, 2006–2007, p. 59).

Maybe that's why, in the high-achieving Netherlands, science teaching is grounded in literacy.

Science and Literacy in the Netherlands

In Dutch science classrooms, literacy is front and center. The textbook plays a central role. Consider the power in the following simple routine: In the Netherlands, specific textbook readings are assigned daily, then introduced by a seemingly dull daily regimen: a five-minute orientation to the text—precisely the kind of purpose-setting "anticipatory set" that ought to be a regular feature of instruction (but usually isn't). When we provide even brief, meaningful background information, we ensure that far more students will understand the text; far more will read with motivation and curiosity and will learn and retain more as a result (Marzano, Pickering, & Pollock, 2001, pp. 92–96). (The crafting of such "orientations" should be high on a team's list of priorities at professional learning community meetings—and during professional development).

After the brief orientation, the readings are interwoven with explanations by the teacher and opportunities to discuss questions related to the reading. Students read for a manageable 20 minutes or so, *as they write* in response to text-related questions. This is followed by a whole-class review of the questions, with the teacher then asking students to revisit and "elaborate" on their initial written responses (Roth & Garnier, 2006–2007, p. 20).

The whole-class review is a crucial step. I'm not sure the average teacher has discovered the magic in this straightforward step of having students review their writings and annotations (even a few minutes after writing, taking notes, or annotating). This invariably promotes deep thought—the ability to see patterns, to make new inferences and connections that they didn't, or couldn't, see before. It's a ripe, simple opportunity to clarify, extend, and refine our thought even further as we "think on paper." This is the "miraculous power" writing has to make us better thinkers (R. D. Walshe in Schmoker, 2006). This simple routine could be used several times per week, in any science course—just as it is in the Netherlands.

Strategic reading, writing, and talking have never been prominent features of U.S. science instruction. How does this affect prospects for scientific learning and careers?

Why We Fail: The Erosion of Literacy

The erosion of literacy is one of the most profound but insidious developments in modern schooling. Until we put literacy at the heart of science instruction, the goal of science learning for all will elude us.

Gomez and Gomez found that students' difficulties with reading textbook materials were among the chief reasons for low performance in science and social studies (2007). Though textbooks continue to line the shelves of most classrooms, actual textbook *reading* is "abandoned early" (2007, p. 225). With each passing year, students fall further behind in their ability to read challenging, content-rich text. No one sounds the alarm, even as teachers cease to even see the textbook as "an active, meaningful ingredient" in science instruction. The current rage for activities "conspires to keep understanding of text below the instructional radar" (2007, p. 228).

In their article on science education, Hapgood and Palincsar note similarly the "impoverished reading diets" on which we put students the moment school begins. Despite what we say, the actual taught curriculum suffers from a crushing "dearth of informational texts" (2006–2007, pp. 56–57). The consequences of this "diet" show up in the later grades.

Zmach and colleagues implore science instructors to make content-based literacy lessons the core of science instruction, right from the beginning. They recommend extensive reading, discussion, and note taking from science texts—with plenty of "modeling, guided practice," and independent practice (2006–2007, pp. 63–65). But we avoid such instruction, starting in the early years. As a result, middle school students have difficulty reading "demanding text . . . [in] their textbooks and content-area materials in science" (p. 62). Rather than redress this situation aggressively, both middle and high school collectively abdicate, as "students engage in *little reading of content texts in secondary classrooms*" (p. 63).

Thus does the American bias against text quietly diminish learning, aptitude, and interest in science, technical, and mathematics careers.

What Real-Life Scientists Say About Reading

Our aversion to demanding text ensures that students will continue to underperform in the content areas (Gomez & Gomez, 2007, p. 225). As we've been seeing, you cannot learn a discipline without being a habitual, close reader in that discipline (Alberts, 2006–2007; McConachie et al., 2006). Such reading—and note taking—is essential to understanding the essence of science (Shanahan & Shanahan, 2008).

Real scientists know this. Let's now listen to two of them—acquaintances of mine—as they share their perspective on the vital (if unfashionable) importance of science textbooks.

An Astronomer's Point of View

Jeff Hall is an astronomer working at Lowell Observatory in Flagstaff, Arizona. He speaks almost reverentially of the role of textbooks in his life as a student and successful scientist.

Where I'm sitting, I can see the spines of some of my favorite textbooks. These books improved my grades greatly by helping me to understand material better. Some of these are real gems, immortal texts I can still learn from . . . they gave me a deep understanding of quantum mechanics, general relativity, thermodynamics, the interaction of light and matter. These are topics that underpin the modern field, and to understand them you have to do *a lot of reading.* (my emphasis)

Scientist don't just "do" science; you can't do scientific work without being a regular reader of scientific articles. Reading textbooks prepares you to read scientific articles. In research, you need to have read enough textbook material to read scientific material with skill, to stay abreast of and maintain currency in the field. Your conversations with other scientists are important, but those conversations simply don't go into as much depth as you get from reading.

For Jeff, reading science textbooks literally "sets the stage for future success in scientific pursuits." This is precisely what it did for another renowned scientist and acquaintance.

An Evolutionary Biologist's Experience

Paul Keim is a popular, world-renowned scientist and a famous local resident, also in Flagstaff, Arizona. An eminent evolutionary biologist at Northern Arizona University, he was the lead researcher who helped crack the Washington, D.C., anthrax case of 2001.

Keim speaks of the complementary power of reading and lectures and of the value that textbook reading had for him when he was a student.

I shape my lectures around the content in the textbooks, so that they reinforce and complement each other, so that the text supports and clarifies my lectures. For students, this approach is invaluable.

Keim doesn't have students read all of the textbook. He wants students to read deeply and slowly, the way he did as a student:

There is too much material in most textbooks. I have them read about 25 percent of the text. The body of facts and concepts they will learn from lectures simply don't stand by themselves. They need to be put in the context of the discipline. How can we talk about the nucleus of a cell without understanding cytoplasm?

The textbook is one of the few places you can go to learn more and in more depth about these concepts; it gives you the total story [my emphasis]. The big downside for those who don't read the text-book is that they don't get the critical supportive details. No matter how effective your lectures are, there is so much good auxiliary material students will miss if they don't read the text.

That vital "auxiliary material," read slowly, gave Keim a crucial advantage when he was a student.

"Slow Reading": An Equalizer

Ironically, textbooks can be either a barrier to learning or an opportunity to catch up or accelerate science learning. Textbooks can be, in Professor Keim's term, true "equalizers"—providing an opportunity for slower students (all students) to catch up if they get behind. As Keim explained,

The information in the textbook provides students the chance to slow down or speed up, to get more details at their own pace. It gives them the chance to catch up if they aren't understanding everything in the lectures. The textbook can be an equalizer for slower students. . . . In college *I would often read only one page in my biochem book at a time*. I had to read and reread the most difficult material. That gave me an advantage, being able to reread parts of the text until I understood it. (my emphasis)

Clearly, it is time we made textbooks a central element of science teaching—starting in the early grades. And we need to teach students the simple strategies for how to read them. This can't be left to chance; we need to model how we would read science texts, several times per week, showing students how we would annotate, how we would reread or refer to graphics in the text to achieve understanding, form arguments, and make connections as we navigate the "lexical density" of science textbooks (Shanahan & Shanahan, 2008, p. 53).

These fairly straightforward activities would have great impact, as would another traditional, underestimated tool we've already discussed: lecture. Executed effectively, lecture complements textbook reading, as it does for Professor Keim. As Bybee and Van Scotter point out, "reading, lecture, and discussion" are among the essential elements for promoting reasoning and scientific literacy (2006–2007, pp. 44–45). For James Trefil (2008), lecture is one of the most powerful, efficient ways to impart a foundation of essential scientific knowledge.

Interactive Lecture

As we've seen, there are tremendous advantages to employing the right amount of lecture in any content area. Interactive lecture can be a "marvel of efficiency" (Silver et al., 2007, p. 26). But done wrong (as it often is), lecture is among the most boring and ineffective practices.

To be effective, interactive lecture has to contain the same routine components described in Chapter 3 and that recur throughout this book: modeling, guided practice, and formative assessment.

I encourage you to revisit the more detailed treatment of interactive lecture in Chapter 3, but here are its essential steps.

• Begin the lecture by providing essential or provocative background knowledge and an overarching unit question or some essential questions.
• Ensure that the lecture stays closely focused on the question.
• Ensure, through guided practice and formative assessment, that students are engaged and on task; do this by circulating, observing, and listening as students take notes and pair up to process each chunk of the lecture.

• Avoid talking for more than seven minutes without giving students an opportunity to connect learning to their essential question or task—to review their notes and pair up to compare their connections and perceptions with others.

• Ensure, in discussions, that all students respond multiple times during the lecture.

• Reteach or clarify whenever checks for understanding indicate that students have not mastered the material in the previous chunk of instruction—and only move on when you feel they are ready.

This model has a lot going for it, including the essential components that are the backbone of any effective lesson. Because it is both interactive and highly effective, it can be a regular staple of instruction—and would therefore have a disproportionately positive impact on learning.

We now know about the importance of content learned through literacy activities and effective interactive lecture. To clarify further, let's now look at how all this fits into the scheme of standards, pacing, and assessment.

Achieving Coherence with Science Standards

Once again, the aim here is not to prescribe or to show the one best way to select and apportion standards. I merely want to simplify and demystify this process that is so critical to achieving common, coherent curriculum. The general process is described in detail in Chapter 3 (which I encourage you to revisit).

Choosing Standards

In brief, start by having each member of your team choose only the most essential 50 percent or so of what is on the standards document. Then, record on a flipchart or whiteboard only those standards that all or most participants agreed on—a much shorter list. As mentioned earlier, this can be a very rewarding moment as teachers see common patterns of agreement and as they realize, at a glance, that they can indeed cover this now-manageable amount of core content and can do it *in sufficient depth*. Fewer standards means there is time to incorporate the higher-order reading, discussion, and writing that we know is essential to content area learning.

Even so, these drastic reductions can make some participants nervous. It never hurts for the facilitator to remind participants that the countries with the highest achievement in science and math teach *fewer than half the number of standards* we have in our bloated documents.

Let's now look at how we might complete this process if we were mapping 6th grade science standards. The same basic approach/procedures would work for 2nd grade science or high school chemistry.

Establishing Pacing

The first thing we would notice is that there are nine pages of standards (in the science standards document I'm looking at). That's way too many. After an initial review, the team would probably agree there are redundancies, vague language, and too many unnecessary details in this highly rated standards document—which was, again, *never field-tested*. For starters, the first two pages contain an unwieldy abundance of terms and directives for "inquiry process" (their unfortunate word for labs and experiments; as we've seen, content area "inquiry" regularly occurs in the context of reading, talking, and writing). As we discuss and list our favorite standards, we would realize that the essential standards from these two pages could be boiled down to the following:

Students will design and/or conduct X number of controlled investigations per unit/grading period. These will incorporate background reading and research; the use of hypotheses, observations, measurement, and record keeping; and communication of results and conclusions in writing and with tables, graphs, and charts.

We then could add this: *all labs and experiments will directly support the science content we are teaching in the unit.*

We just eliminated about a page and a half of bloat from the state standards. We did it without sacrificing essence while *adding* clarity, concision, and connection to essential content, not to mention that the members of our 6th grade team are far more apt to actually teach such short, essential lists of standards and less apt to revert to the "self-selected jumble" (Rosenholtz, 1991) that results from foisting unrealistically long, untested lists of standards on practitioners (Marzano, 2003).

One strand down, six to go. One of them is "history and nature of science." It mentions numerous major scientists and important discoveries. We know we'll never get around to this many, so we decide to learn about *only half* of them and to teach only *two scientists and their allied discoveries* for each of the five remaining major content units (life science, environmental science, physical science, earth science, and space science).

We must now divide the five remaining strands by grading periods. Here, too, we decide to reduce the number of topics in each strand by about half—and by even more in physical science (which we thought had far too much material). We end up eliminating enough material from physical science to teach *both* physical science *and some* earth science during 3rd quarter. We will teach the remainder of earth science and the essential standards for the last strand—space science—during 4th quarter. So our general standards map looks something like this:

- First quarter: essential topics and content/units for life science.
- Second quarter: essential topics and content/units for environmental science.

• Third quarter: essential topics and content/units for physical science, with some earth science.

• Fourth quarter: essential topics and content/units for earth science and space science.

For all of the above two- to four-week units, we will provide only the most appropriate, well-integrated labs and experiments and two one- to two-day studies of important scientists or major scientific movements and discoveries (using online resources found by the team).

Simple. But such processes ensure that we'll make enormous strides toward guaranteed and viable curriculum. If we complete them with a review of 5th and 7th grade science curriculum—to fill in any important gaps and reduce redundancy—we're even better off. We'll increase the odds that a good, coherent curriculum is actually taught, with plenty of room for in-depth reading, writing, and discussion about essential concepts and topics.

But to ensure that these good things actually occur, we have to do one more thing: develop common assessments for each grading period and unit.

Creating Assessments

End-of-grading-period assessments may include a certain amount of multiple-choice items. But at least half of our assessments will consist of good essay-response questions that give students the opportunity to (once again) argue, explain, infer, draw their own conclusions, and synthesize the views found in conflicting source documents (Conley, 2007, p. 24). These assessment questions should be given *before the unit or grading period*—not at the end. They create the form and purpose for each unit while piquing curiosity and interest in the lectures, reading assignments, discussions, and lab activities.

There is no reason that such assessments could not be conducted over two or more days, with access to books, readings, outlines, and lecture notes—in an open-book format. This is because such assessments are not an interruption to learning; the reading, review, and writing are richly educational experiences in and of themselves. Much more of our assessment should be conducted in this fashion. (We'll discuss efficient grading practices in a moment.)

If we're smart, we will literally and repeatedly take students through the steps of how to prepare for truly "educative assessments" (Wiggins, 1998) by modeling and providing supervised practice exercises as we check their understanding and mastery of these moves so essential to success in college or careers.

These written assessments can also be the basis for the quarterly data review: The administrator or teacher leader can simply ask the team

1. How many students succeeded on each end-of-unit and/or end-of-grading-period assessment, and

2. For areas of weakness that need to be worked on in the subsequent grading period (see Schmoker, 2006, pp. 130–33).

To get a clearer look still, let's examine a few sample questions for one grading period and for the major units within the grading period.

Sample Unit Questions and Writing Assignments

Let's assume that during the first grading period, the first of the three units covered in life science will focus on cells—their structure and function, and the differences between plant and animal cells. *Up front*, students will be given the tasks they will need to complete both their end-of-unit and end-of-grading-period assessments. They will know that there will only be a limited number of multiple-choice items on the tests and that half or more of the exam questions will be composed of writing prompts like the following:

- Explain and illustrate cellular structures and functions based on reading and lecture notes, with original or personal observations, insights, and connections. (The teacher will clarify and model "observations, insights, and connections" *multiple times* during the unit.)
- Explain and illustrate essential similarities and differences between plant and animal cells.
- Read two opposing arguments on a past or present issue or problem related to cells/cell research (e.g., stem cells, pharmaceuticals) and annotate them. Take a position on this issue. Be sure to also refer to what you learned in this unit on cells.

Each of these writing activities quite naturally incorporates inferencing, drawing conclusions, supporting arguments with evidence, and reconciling conflicting source documents.

As an option, on each common assessment (per unit or grading period) we might require students to make arguments and connections with respect to previous units (e.g., linking life science and physical science, or earth and environmental science). To prepare for these assessments, we would be sure to give students ample opportunities to write from their readings and lecture notes. All of these processes would of course be taught with lessons that included modeling, guided practice, and formative assessment. To help students even further, we would take them carefully through exemplars of such written work from previous year's students (with names blacked out). This would be done all year, every year.

As we saw in social studies, we could have students complete one or two more extended essays each semester. This could be done by simply having students choose one end-of-unit question and expand it into a two- to five-page paper (depending on grade level), with the requirement for them to research and integrate a given number of other sources. In a moment, we'll see how current articles could be a part of this. *Even two such papers, each year,* in every science course, would be excellent preparation for the demands of college science or a science career.

Again, as we saw in social studies, we cannot expect science teachers to be English teachers. Most short writing assignments could be graded by walking around and checking off good-faith or satisfactory efforts; longer, more formal papers would be graded primarily for content, clarity, and logic—not the finer points of writing or perfect grammar and mechanics. (See discussion of this and a simplified rubric for social studies and science in Chapter 3.)

Once standards are mapped and assessments are developed, it is time for the next seemingly "boring, pedestrian" (Collins, 2001a, p. 142) step that is in fact enormously productive: selecting, as a team, the best pages from the textbook and from common supplemental readings to go along with each major unit.

Common Readings: Textbook Pages

The preceding elements provide the general infrastructure for good science instruction. Because they reduce and clarify science standards, they decrease anxiety and give teachers confidence that their students are enjoying a coherent, literacy-rich program of study. All can now move forward knowing that students will learn essential, common content, regardless of which teacher they have. But the next step is no less critical (though it is seldom taken seriously).

Choosing Pages

Teams of teachers must go through their textbooks, carefully selecting which pages students should read (not too much now; sometimes two or three pages will suffice). Then they should collect and assemble a core of supplemental texts and articles that support the major units and standards (more on this in a moment).

We would continue to do this in team meetings, as we build and align a strong, focused curriculum with plenty of content learning, reading, writing, and discussion, and the right amount of meaningful lab and hands-on activities.

And there we go. Even crude attempts to implement the above "infrastructure" of science instruction will pay enormous dividends and represent a vast improvement over business as usual.

But we should also institutionalize and enhance an exciting element already discussed in social studies: the inclusion of supplementary and current science readings. Once again: I am as excited about the general payoff this will have for stimulating interest and success in schooling as anything on the horizon. I believe it should make up as much as 20 percent of the curriculum (inclusive of discussion and writing). That's a hefty amount, I know. Let me make the argument for it now.

Choosing Supplementary Texts

Every week or two, I'd like to see students read and discuss articles about scientific discoveries and controversies. These would be collected from science journals and newsmagazines and from online sources. Ideally, they would connect to the science content students are studying. Some of these texts might have enduring value and become part of the formal curriculum, used for years.

I wouldn't insist that current articles would always have to connect to the unit being studied. After all, science and science articles in any sphere connect to the other sciences and scientific topics. And, as we'll see in a moment, almost any science article offers readers an opportunity to exercise modes of thinking common to all scientific work.

Finally, interesting current articles about late-breaking discoveries have the power of "now"; they often focus on timely, urgent issues of interest. I think that 10 to 20 percent of the curriculum should be focused on such readings, with discussion and writing. I can't imagine a better way to imbue scientific studies with excitement and relevance.

Don't worry that there isn't enough time for this. If we scrap the extraneous (versus essential) standards, along with the movies, worksheets, and the less-essential labs and activities, we will open up more than enough time to have students reading, talking, and writing about the content from their textbooks and the abundance of fascinating articles available about exciting new developments in science. As Hapgood and Palincsar found, students are indeed "eager to talk, read, and write" about science topics. They love to "compare their thinking with other's thinking"—if we set the stage for it (2006–2007, p. 56). This component could do more to promote interest in science and promote the goals of scientific and technical careers than anything done to date, and the materials for doing this are readily available.

Kelly Gallagher (2009) has made close, analytical reading of *Newsweek* a weekly staple of instruction in his high school English courses. His mission is to help students to become more informed, thoughtful, and articulate. This weekly exercise helps ensure that they will be.

Articles for Elementary School Students

Newsweek has real merits for secondary students, but there are several good sources more appropriate for the younger grades. In the social studies chapter, I described *TIME for Kids, Junior Scholastic,* and other excellent resources for younger students. *TIME for Kids* also contains many good science-related articles. As I previously noted, one recent article addressed the possible reasons for the depletion of tiger populations; another looked at earthquakes (in Haiti and Chile). These were written for 2nd and 3rd graders. Each article is written in clear, readable prose, packed with the kinds of interesting facts and statistics upon which scientific thinking depends. *Kid Biz/ Achieve 3000* is another good resource that translates recent newspaper and magazine articles into language appropriate for different grade levels.

Again, a caution: *Please ignore the ever-present questions, activities, and worksheets that always accompany such materials—they are seldom worth your time. Instead, simply have students read carefully to argue, infer, and make their own connections and conclusions as they read, underline, and annotate.*

Of course, there are many other good resources. Two that I've mentioned previously and that I think are especially helpful are ProCon.org and *The Week.*

ProCon.org is an excellent, free source for any teacher, and certainly for the science teacher. In its science and technology section, you will find abundant materials arguing both sides of issues like the following:

- Alternative energy versus fossil fuels
- Are cell phones safe?
- Is nuclear power practical?

For many of the topics, you can click to related pages. For example, the alternative energy page contains links to many short, readable arguments for and against the use of biofuels and nuclear, solar, and hydrogen power. Each topic also has a "one-minute overview" that provides background for the issue in clear, easy-to-read language. With a click, you can review an "expanded background" for each topic. These would be perfect to construct anticipatory sets and pique student curiosity. Below this overview are 9 or 10 short, argumentative paragraphs in each of two columns—"pro" and "con." Each summarizes the important facts or conclusions from one article; citations for each article are listed below (if students want to look them up online). But by themselves, every one of these clear, well-written scientific argumentative paragraphs provides students with abundant opportunities to learn essential content, read closely to make inferences, synthesize competing claims, analyze arguments, and reach conclusions. The format itself is compelling: students have a chance to see the arguments in close juxtaposition, making comparison and synthesis easier. I highly recommend this resource.

Another source of good articles for science courses that I love to recommend is *The Week* (a relative newcomer in the weekly news-magazine category). Once students reach the upper elementary grades (especially if they've done some regular nonfiction reading in the early grades), they are more than up to reading the high-interest science articles from *The Week*, which I discussed at length in the last chapter.

The Week contains excellent science and health articles one page or shorter in length. The "Health and Science" page typically contains about four short, readable pieces. They are consistently arresting and full of potential to spark an interest in science. Each piece stimulates scientific thinking and demystifies the essential patterns always found in scientific studies.

In one issue from May 1, 2009, I found interesting recent scientific discoveries about

- The myth of the multitasker,
- The academic benefits of chewing gum, and
- How Facebook use may adversely affect students' grades.

In all of these pieces—indeed in science articles from any source—we run into the same recurrent patterns and opportunities for discussion, analytic thought, and writing:

- Most of the pieces reflect the interesting and recurring issue of *cause vs. correlation,* which students will enjoy debating. (Is gum chewing the cause of higher grades, or do smart kids like to chew gum? Does Facebook use cause lower grades, or do underachieving students just spend more time on Facebook?)

- All of the brief articles admit (at least implicitly) that many late-breaking discoveries are inconclusive about root causes. (For example, in the gum-chewing piece, some scientists speculate that chewing gum stimulates mental activity because it promotes blood flow in the region of the brain . . . *but they have no proof.*)

- All three pieces exhibit another common pattern in science articles: they invite analysis and debate about *the way the studies were designed.* For example, multitaskers in the one study were identified as those who merely happen to use the most different kinds of technology; nothing is said about using them simultaneously. Taught to read carefully, many students will ask: Is this really the best way to identify "multitaskers"?

- All the articles invite us to think and discuss scientifically, to see connections among science disciplines. The gum-chewing article has implications for both chemistry and biology, and the Facebook article connects both behavioral and biological/neurological science.

These articles are based on serious, well-funded science work. But they exhibit the range and appeal of such studies in a way that is bound to promote interest in students' science courses and in scientific and technical careers.

Frequently, there are also well-written single-page articles in *The Week* on a major scientific issue. I am looking at one on nuclear energy. I will now use it to describe how to model and teach effective reading of such articles—or a textbook, for that matter. Any teacher could learn to do this effectively. And such instruction would demystify such intellectual work and the (quite straightforward) art of reading nonfiction closely and critically.

Close Reading: A Science Article

I would start every weekly lesson carefully reading the first paragraph or two out loud, stopping whenever I felt it beneficial to reread, and even dramatize as I stop to weigh a phrase or sentence. I would note, for instance, that this article tells me the United States has gone "30 years without building a new nuclear plant" but is now "preparing to build as many as 29 in the next several years." I would say to my class:

> This gets my attention. Does it get yours? Why did we wait so long to build more plants—and then decide to build so many so fast? I have always had mixed feelings about nuclear power. [I might briefly share my knowledge of the Three Mile Island and Chernobyl incidents, and use this as an opportunity to explain how previous knowledge helps us to evaluate current arguments and think critically about what we read.] I want to read on to see if the article addresses my concerns or adds anything new that might change my opinion.

In the next line, I read that nuclear plants "emit no greenhouse gases."

> None? Zero? I didn't know this. That's great, but that leaves the issue of nuclear waste, which is also very dangerous. I mean, that has to be why we haven't been building new plants all these years. So I will read the rest of this article—as should you—for the answer to this question: Is it safer to build such plants now than it used to be? Do we know new ways to get rid of harmful nuclear waste? With these questions in mind, I will read these arguments very carefully.

I might go on to read another portion of the article that tells us that thanks to nuclear power, the United States now releases 190 million fewer tons of carbon dioxide per year. I might say:

> Sounds great, but I'm wondering—relative to what? What is the total amount of carbon dioxide that enters the atmosphere each year? Is 190 million tons a drop in the global bucket or a sizeable proportion?

Here students are learning another core intellectual habit—that numbers are indispensable in many arguments but must always be looked at carefully. Because numbers have such persuasive power, we have to be somewhat on our guard: The worth of any number or statistic is almost always relative—important only with respect to other numbers or values.

Close Reading of the Textbook

We would do the same kind of close, careful reading if we were reading a science text. According to Shanahan and Shanahan, science textbooks and articles must be read closely and carefully. In science, even more than in most subjects, we need to recognize the close interdependence between words and graphics. To understand the concepts found in science textbooks, readers must do something simple but somewhat unnatural: we must often reread and alternate—many times if necessary—between the written text and any illustrations or statistical tables. In this way, as one scientist pointed out, students "learn the essence of science" (Shanahan & Shanahan, 2008, p. 54).

These are the simple but essential operations that mature adult readers perform automatically to master difficult, complex material. But students don't realize early enough that even adults pause, many times, to reread a sentence or paragraph or refer to an illustration several times—in order to understand it.

If we want *not some but all students* to learn science, we need to repeatedly model, encourage, remind, and reinforce these simple operations of thoughtful reading every year in *all* science classes. Then, as with any good lesson, we need to follow up such modeling with opportunities for guided practice. Let them read the next paragraph or two, annotate or scribble some notes or reflections, and then share those with each other in pairs. This prepares and gives them confidence for the next important step: to share their now much clearer, more refined thoughts in whole-class discussions—whether it is about molecular theory or the pros and cons of wind energy. (Again, I would encourage you to revisit and integrate the use of the two templates in Chapter 3, which pertain to virtually any lesson or learning target in a good curriculum.)

If we do such simple things, repeatedly, from the earliest grades, students *will learn* to read and think and articulate with increasing skill and sophistication. But they must also write, for writing takes students to even higher levels of clarity and precision in their powers of thought.

Writing in Science

As often as possible, every close reading or discussion should include or end with some opportunity—if even for just a few minutes—to summarize, argue, or respond to a question in writing. It is in writing that students have a chance to convert what they have learned from reading and talking into more coherent, logical, and precise thought and language. In writing, new thoughts are often born, thoughts that build on the insights already gleaned from reading and talking. Writing takes thinking to the next level (see Schmoker, 2006, Chapter 5).

Doug Reeves (2008) is a longtime champion of writing in the content areas. His Leadership and Learning Center conducted a research study showing that writing and note taking, consistently implemented, contribute tremendously to learning science content. In schools where writing and note taking were rarely implemented in science classes, approximately 25 percent of students scored proficient or higher on state assessments. But in schools where writing and note taking were consistently implemented by science teachers, 79 percent scored at the proficient level. Writing matters—hugely.

With this much at stake, students should regularly write short pieces, maybe one or two brief paragraphs. They might simply cite a few notes or annotations from the text to formulate an argument or two based on the understanding they have acquired from close reading and discussion.

It is also critical for science students to write at least two longer papers each year—their length increasing at each grade level. By high school, these should be three to five typewritten pages— mostly completed in class, where we can monitor, guide, and check for understanding to ensure success. As Conley (2005) found, liberal amounts of such writing could have more of an impact on college readiness than any single measure we could take.

Science teachers are not English teachers—and vice versa. In science, the emphasis should be on producing a sound, readable paper that will be evaluated primarily for clarity and content—for the student's ability to cite written sources to support a scientific argument or conclusion with evidence. The finer points of writing can be left to the language arts teacher.

• • •

Again, the suggestions here are not intended to be exhaustive, but rather to bring us back to the surefire elements that should be the focus of the great majority of science instruction: close reading and discussion, interactive lecture, regular reading and discussion of current science articles, writing, and a reasonable number of science labs and experiments tied directly to the content being learned.

These simple elements should constitute the operative core of science instruction, on which our staff development and team meetings should consistently focus. If they do, we will make great strides toward ensuring a high-quality science education for all.

Let's now look at one of the critical underpinnings of scientific thought and exploration—mathematics.

Making Math Meaningful

It is not yet clear whether the best option for all is the historic algebra-based mainstream that is animated primarily by the power of abstraction. . . . Teachers need to focus on the interplay of numbers and words, especially on expressing quantitative relationships in meaningful sentences . . . to make mathematics meaningful, the three Rs must be well blended in each student's mind.

Lynn Steen

• • •

I can no longer imagine teaching math without making writing an integral aspect of students' learning.

Marilyn Burns

Mathematics is *pervasive*. If we want all students to become confident, comfortable, knowledgeable users of math, we need to ensure that math curriculum is coherent, that it is always taught with the same powerful elements of good lessons we've been looking at in every chapter, and that it is infused with literacy.

As with language arts, math standards deserve a hard, fresh look. As currently written, do math standards, including the national standards, take us closer to the goal of meaningful, practical math mastery for all? When the political dust settles, will we be teaching the right standards in the right amount—those with strong links to the real world of the 21st century?

Math: Are We Teaching the Right Stuff?

This discussion has to be seen against math's acknowledged difficulty and power to diminish students' academic prospects. More students fail in math than any other subject (Singham, 2005; Steen, 2007), a fact which contributes disproportionately to academic frustration and dropout rates. Many have begun to ask how much sense it makes to require all students to learn the most abstract, algebra-based mathematics, especially if it can't be shown to have any genuine connection to the workplace (Meier, 2010; Steen, 2007; Wolk, 2010). Urban educator and author Deborah Meier provocatively suggests,

> It might be fruitful to question the assumption that "everyone" must take advanced algebra . . . if the trend continues to make mastering algebra a roadblock to further study. Why don't we remove the roadblock instead? (2010, p. 23)

As we embark on yet another (i.e. national) standards movement, we should continue to examine not only the number but the *nature* of math standards—the conventional "algebra-based mainstream" that we seem hesitant to honestly scrutinize. Does traditional math coursework truly prepare students for life, or for the kinds of work they encounter in their careers—even scientific and high-tech careers? Or would different math standards—and course requirements—be more meaningful? The answers to these questions could have significant positive consequences.

The need for mathematical thinking has never been greater. And for math to have meaning, "the interplay of numbers and words," or literacy, must become a central feature of math education (Steen,

2007, p. 10). To address these issues, perhaps the first order of business is to reduce the sheer number of standards.

Simplifying Math Standards

Stanford's R. James Milgram is convinced that the "unbelievable success" of the highest-achieving countries in math can be directly attributed to the fact that they teach only a few math topics—intensely—each year (in De Vise, 2006). In the United States, our typical standards documents contain about 50 topics per grade level. Imagine how much more in-depth application—and student success—would be possible if we reduced our standards (De Vise, 2006). In Chapter 2, we saw evidence and examples of schools that made the courageous move to greatly reduce their math standards—and saw dramatic increases in achievement as a result.

For decades, Michigan State University professor William Schmidt has been at the forefront of efforts to reduce the number of U.S. educational standards and to teach them more meaningfully. Good standards, he writes, "need to focus on a small enough number of topics so that teachers can spend *months, not days*, on them" (2008, p. 22, my emphasis). Right now, the penchant in the United States for packing each grade level with overlapping topics makes that impossible. As Schmidt wrote recently, "everything is covered everywhere" (2008, p. 23). This profusion of standards forces each teacher to make ad-hoc selections from their standards documents, which produces the phenomenon we know so well: "great variability among courses with the same title" (2008, p. 24). Will the new national standards put an end to this? My contacts in major math organizations aren't so sure.

We need to teach a smaller number of the most essential standards so that we can teach them more deeply and meaningfully. Yet we also need to move incrementally, and courageously, to increase the proportion of math standards that have strong, *visible* connections to meaning and application—links that will motivate students to press on when discouraged. Without this, math will continue to be "the ultimate exercise in deferred gratification" (Steen, 2007, p. 12).

Breaking the Silence:
The Algebra-Based Mainstream

Lynn Steen is among our wisest and most esteemed math educators. He is also among a growing cadre who question the essential core of current math standards. In the lead article for *Educational Leadership*'s "Making Math Count" issue, he drops this bomb: "It is not yet clear whether the best option for all is the historic algebra-based mainstream that is animated primarily by the power of 'abstraction'" (2007, p. 12). Abstraction is the enemy, he observes: "As the level of abstraction increases . . . links to meaning fade." As meaning fades, so does motivation to learn, understanding, course success, and—for many—college prospects.

Mano Singham, a professor at Case Western Reserve University, observes that math has "the lowest pass rates in proficiency tests for all ethnic groups" (2005, p. 84). In Cleveland, Ohio, where he lives, only 20 percent of students pass the state math exam the first time they take it (p. 15).

The question we have to ask is: For all this academic pain, is there a commensurate amount of real-world gain—beyond school? Here's where it gets interesting.

Math "in the Real World"

In "Solving Problems in the Real World" (1997), Henry Pollack demonstrates that the working world does indeed require more complex mathematical thinking and problem solving than ever. *But these seldom involve the use of algebra or advanced mathematics.* If we really wanted to prepare students for the mathematical demands of current and future careers, it would make more sense to give them more opportunities to apply fairly basic math to complex situations and problems like those they will face in the workplace.

Steen concurs. In the real world, students actually need *less* abstract, advanced math; they need *more* elementary and middle school math. As he points out (and as my interviews with math and science professionals confirm), life and work increasingly present us with challenging, complex problems that require mathematical savvy and solutions. The real world requires "sophisticated thinking with elementary skills (for example, arithmetic, percentages, ratios)" (Steen, 2007, p. 13). Students don't need to learn more advanced algorithms that they'll never use, even as engineers or scientists. What they *do* need are far more frequent opportunities to practice and apply "simple skills" as they tackle issues like "global warming, college tuition and gas prices . . . data-rich topics that can also challenge them with surprising complications" (Steen, 2007, p. 13).

We've postponed this reckoning with meaning for decades. Arnold Packer minces no words: Schools should abandon a "failed [math] curriculum" that insists on advanced coursework but "relegates applications to an afterthought" (1997, pp. 138–139). Packer found that only 4 percent of the population—pure mathematicians, astronomers, physicists, and only a tiny subset of engineers—uses advanced algebraic concepts in their work. But how much math do even these high-caliber professionals use?

Who Needs Advanced Math?

* * *

To force every student to study higher-order math, whether or not . . . they will ever use it in life after school, is cruel and unusual punishment.

Ron Wolk

* * *

I wonder how many people paid serious attention to a startling set of figures about math in the workplace in a recent *Education*

Week report. For starters, about 80 percent of the overall workforce, including those in the highest-paying, most prestigious careers, will *never use anything beyond addition, subtraction, multiplication, and division.* Eighty percent! Even among those in the most lucrative, fastest-growing, "upper white collar" careers, only 30 percent will ever use any Algebra I. And only 14 percent of that highly educated subgroup will use *any* Algebra II. Overall, *less than 5 percent of the workforce* will make extensive use of Algebra II or other advanced courses (Cavanagh, 2007).

One wonders, would it be wiser to replace some of our advanced courses with applied math, statistics, or data analysis of the kind that actually gets used in the working world? And how wise is it to make Algebra II the new standard for college entry or graduation (as many states have now done)? (I never took Algebra II myself, nor did many of my most successful, college-educated friends.)

The next question is, of those in math- and science-related careers, *how much* do they use algebra or more advanced coursework in the workplace?

How Much Algebra?

I have spoken with or interviewed dozens of people who took advanced algebra, trigonometry, or calculus in their postsecondary training, as required by high school and college programs. This group includes nurses, tradespeople, scientists, and lots of engineers. They worked in nuclear power plants, laboratories, hospitals, and the defense and aerospace industries. All of them spent enormous amounts of time sweating their way through difficult, abstract courses in high school and college, with little or no explanation for how or if what they learned would ever apply to their work. To a person, they were emphatic in telling me that they rarely, if ever, used such advanced math operations on the job. Several told me that the algebraic formulas they did use—so rarely—were usually fairly simple; anyone could be taught them on the job, using a calculator.

Not so many years ago, my uncle, Leo Daoust, retired from Boeing in Seattle, Washington. He was one of the highest-ranking engineers in the entire company. He told me that in all those years, he seldom used advanced levels of college math. In fact, he never went to college.

These interviews confirm the findings of the *Education Week* report, as well as the conclusions of educators like Packer and Steen.

What About the Future?

Could the demand for advanced math coursework increase in the future? Perhaps. That's why we should continue to ensure that students receive a good grounding in the most essential, practical math standards—up through algebra and geometry. But we should also begin the work of reducing the amount of standards, starting with the most abstract, algebra-based operations that the math and science professions *cannot identify as important to high-tech work.* If some of these operations become important to math- and science-related work, surely they will let us know. And we'll be glad to restore them to the curriculum, with this vital difference: We'll be able to tell students how they apply in the real world.

Colleges and engineering departments should be introspective here as well, and willing to look at how much of their curriculum is a rite of passage rather than actual career preparation. And we shouldn't be shy about telling students that a wide range of college majors only require a minimum amount of fairly basic math courses.

At the state and national levels, those who write math standards should begin the important work of asking hard questions and then reducing, carefully and circumspectly, the proportion of the most abstract, algebra-based mathematics—unless they can truly be justified by those in math-related professions. And, I believe, states should suspend the requirement for Algebra II until we reexamine the need for it. We may want to replace it with a requirement for students to take high-quality applied math and statistics courses (which we should be building and piloting—immediately).

Fortunately, schools and districts don't have to wait until these issues are fully addressed (as we wait to see if the national standards will promote progress in these areas).

Schools and Districts: What to Do *Now*?

The following adjustments could be implemented immediately and with great benefits.

Have teams create leaner standards maps for every math course at every grade level. Regardless of what the national standards are, we should aim to reduce the standards to an amount that is only about 50 percent of our current state standards. Chapter 3 presents a simple process for doing this, along with compelling evidence that any good-faith, collective attempt to significantly reduce standards both adds quality and increases test scores—significantly. Moreover, and as we've seen in every chapter of this book, when we reduce standards, we increase the odds of a guaranteed and viable curriculum—one that allows for sufficient depth and is *actually taught*. This is arguably the factor that most affects student learning and test scores (Marzano, 2003).

Once we have built our common standards maps, we need to avail ourselves of the most obvious and effective instructional strategies.

Become truly obsessive about the use of effective teaching strategies in all K–12 math courses. In a discipline that has the highest failure rates, every math department should initiate a campaign to clarify, repeat, and monitor implementation of the routine components of effective instruction we've described throughout this book. If all math teachers began to assiduously implement modeling, guided practice, and checks for understanding—in every lesson—the impact would be dramatic. Dylan Wiliam calculates that this alone would cause the United States to rise to the top five in international rankings of math achievement (Wiliam, 2007, p. 189).

Systematically begin to create and integrate opportunities for students to more deeply understand and apply

essential math concepts. Teams of math teachers should routinely work to identify and develop applications and opportunities for thought and analysis for as many of their (much-reduced) math concepts as possible. This would be greatly enhanced by the following two recommendations:

1. Recruit math and science professionals to help math teachers conduct a systematic review of math standards to determine which ones are truly needed in the workplace and which aren't. They can also tell us what's missing (applied statistics? probability?) and suggest workplace problems and simulations that would make math real for students. All of this would be enhanced by the integration of literacy.

2. Integrate reading, writing, and discussion into problem solving, application, and interpretation. In a moment, we'll see how close reading and writing promote mathematical reasoning and thinking skills. We should routinely provide opportunities for students to use writing to problem solve, defend solutions, and interpret charts, graphs, tables, and other sets of data.

The Interplay of Numbers and Words

To make math more meaningful, we must redouble our efforts to incorporate all three Rs into the math curriculum. For Steen, literacy—that is, the first two Rs—is the missing key to better math education. Deep, practical learning depends upon the reciprocal "interplay of numbers and words, especially on expressing quantitative relationships in meaningful sentences" (Steen, 2007, p. 10). This connection between math and literacy becomes clearer in Steen's simple formulation that all mathematics has two fundamental aspects: calculation and interpretation. The greater of these is interpretation. For numbers and algorithms to have meaning and worth, they must be interpreted and applied to "serve human purposes" (p. 10). To become effective citizens and workers, students must learn to interpret both numbers and text, in combination, in both math textbooks and real-world documents. Students need frequent opportunities to express their quantitative interpretations in arguments and proposals. Such *literate/mathematical thinkers* are precisely what employers seek—those who can read, speak, write, and communicate for practical purposes "in the natural and social sciences" (Steen, 2007, p. 11). Students would enjoy this and would enjoy the chance to make "quantitative arguments" that reveal the power in numbers.

Quantitative Arguments in Every Subject

Math is a marvel of order and elegance. But its primary purpose, writes Steen, is to help us make and dismantle oral and written "quantitative or logical arguments." These arguments touch on every aspect of our lives: "Virtually every subject taught in school is amenable to some use of quantitative or logical arguments that tie evidence to conclusions" (2007, p. 12).

Numbers are a central element in popular or professional books and articles. As students read and respond to quantitative arguments, they can hone those habits of mind mentioned throughout this book—as they argue, problem solve, make inferences, and resolve conflicting views and findings. Arguments often stand or fall on the use of numbers and statistics, which writers employ to advance their proposals, predictions, and "interpretations." These are quantitative arguments.

A facility with numbers helps us to more accurately weigh, convey, and synthesize demographic factors; understand elections; determine who or what to vote for; effectively market goods and services; gauge a nation's social or political health; make predictions; evaluate campaign pledges, policies, and promises; or take intelligent risks on a stock or a professional athlete. We need numbers to make and monitor intelligent budgets, to determine how much economic pain we can sustain as we attempt to reduce greenhouse gases, and to predict when employment will begin to rise and in which occupations.

Once again, the above problems and challenges *seldom require advanced algebra-based mathematics*. They depend more on our ability to skillfully read, write, and interpret quantities, percentages, ratios, and trends. Such operations also routinely buttress quantitative arguments we encounter in popular publications that inform current debates about the pressing social, political, and technological issues of our time. Shouldn't students have opportunities to read and discuss such math-rich documents?

Quantitative Arguments in Popular Nonfiction

I'm looking at two bestselling books on my side table that have had a considerable influence on policy and thought on major current issues. Both are written in clear, readable prose. And both are packed with "quantitative arguments" that make *sophisticated* use of *simple* math operations to solve problems in the social, natural, and physical sciences.

Fareed Zakaria's *The Post-American World* (2008) argues that though the United States may be on the decline, the country and the world in general may be better off as a result. Globalization, he argues, is the reason for these developments. Almost every page of the book contains simple numbers and statistics that support his argument. He shows us, for instance, that due to global trade, world poverty has fallen from 40 percent of the population in 1981 to 18 percent in 2004, and is projected to go down to 12 percent by 2015. A few pages later, Zakaria cites sources showing that there has been about a 60 percent reduction in global warfare since the 1980s. That means we're probably now living in the most peaceful era in recorded history.

Such arguments bring the value of numbers, graphs, and trend lines alive. They can be springboards for additional questions, calculations, and interpretations. For example, how reliable are these figures? Can we attribute these improvements solely to global trade?

Thomas Friedman's *Hot, Flat and Crowded* (2008) is a cornucopia of interesting numbers, trends, fractions, and percentages that add torque to his arguments about the need and opportunity to create a more energy-efficient world. For instance, by comparing tables showing polling data and the price of oil in Russia, he comes to some interesting conclusions about the rise of petro-dictators. That is, when oil was $20 a barrel, Vladimir Putin's approval rating was about 20 percent; when it was $100 a barrel (thus raising the average Russian's standard of living), Putin's approval ratings approached 100 percent (2008).

You don't figure such things out by using higher math; you reach these conclusions by making creative, continuous use of conventional operations—quantitative arguments—to solve relevant problems.

Friedman's book is filled with numbers and statistics arguing that committed efforts will lead to astonishing breakthroughs. For example, he notes that air conditioners, once thought to have reached the limits of efficiency, are now two-thirds more efficient than they were only 10 years ago. There are other figures showing each sector of the economy as a percentage of the total energy pie (transportation tops the list at 30 percent) and how concerted efforts in the most high-leverage areas would increase oil reserves, reduce carbon, and create a greener and more vibrant economy.

Again, such numbers are most powerful in that they afford us with opportunities to extrapolate from them—to calculate and extend our own interpretations for practical purposes. This is how we acquire an appreciation of math's rich and pervasive implications and applications.

Students won't typically read whole books in math classes. But there is no reason they can't be given excerpts or have 15–20 opportunities per year to read current articles that let them see numbers in action. Such reading should always start with modeling and teaching students how to read documents.

Quantitative Arguments with Current Articles

As I write this, I am looking at an article in my local paper about what it would cost to provide health insurance for the uninsured in my state. I find that the current price of health care in the United States is now $2.4 trillion. Whenever I use an article like this in class, I always model for students how, with any such number, I would ask: Is 2.4 trillion a lot? How do we know? Compared to what? How does it compare to the overall economy—what percentage or fraction does it represent? (Answer: about one-sixth.) Students get a kick out of knowing that the U.S. economy is about $16 trillion. And wouldn't it be interesting to know how this percentage compares to *other* countries' total economies?

I go on to read that health care is supposed to increase from about $13,000 to about $30,000 in the next 10 years for a family of four (and how might national health care affect this?). I might then ask pairs or groups of students to figure out how that compares to expected increases in wages and inflation (using additional information that I might provide).

Please don't tell me students don't care about such issues and wouldn't enjoy tackling such problems in pairs or small groups every week or two. If we share such thoughts and think aloud with our students and let them think on paper and then compare their thoughts in pairs, they will acquire a deeper sense of urgent issues—while having fun in the bargain.

Again, success here hinges on teams of teachers sharing the work of collecting 15–20 such articles for every grade level. Many of these could be used for several years (becoming part of the team's permanent or semi-permanent collection). These could be culled from the local newspaper or from magazines like *TIME for Kids,*

Junior Scholastic, Kid Biz, Newsweek, or *The Week.* (We saw how helpful these can be in previous chapters.)

Such articles, as we've seen, are full of quantitative arguments:
comparative earthquake magnitudes, population and poverty statistics, casualty rates, amounts of money spent on foreign aid. Students
can discuss, debate, extrapolate from, and write about these.

Quantitative Arguments Using Raw Data

Among the most interesting documents we can have students
interpret in math are sets of data. George Hillocks, a pioneer in
meta-analysis, gave great importance to the word "inquiry." For
him, inquiry occurred when students were given documents con-
taining raw information or data and were then asked to develop
their own arguments from these data (Hillocks, 1987).

Data can provide rich opportunities for real-world mathematical
thinking. Students could be asked to make inferences, support arguments, and draw conclusions using sources like these:

• Tables showing week-over-week movie sales and production
costs (gathered from newspapers). Students could identify patterns
or make sales projections based on opening week or by genre (drama,
comedy, action). What implications might this have for marketing
or investment in the movie industry?

• Demographic and quality-of-life statistics for various cities,
states, and countries (maybe even within a given continent). Students could compare and evaluate data for varying criteria—overall
quality of life, security, income, culture, et cetera.

• Statistics on athletes. For example, pick two players at the
same position, analyze their stats, and come up with a formula to
determine and defend what you think they are worth. Or have students review statistics to suggest a plausible, mutually beneficial
trade between teams.

We should always be on the lookout for opportunities for students to play around with numbers to make quantitative arguments: to solve problems, identify implications, or reach original, actionable conclusions. We can build up our collections of such scenarios by consulting with working professionals in the community.

Again, the small price for generating such interest and engagement is the team's commitment to building a collection of intriguing problems, questions, articles, graphs, tables, trends, and demographic data. Such resources are a great way to get students analyzing and developing their own quantitative arguments, graphs, and written explanations in ways that transfer readily to the modern workplace. Why not make such work a key aspect of staff development and its funding?

Let's now look more closely at the importance of teaching and modeling how to read actual math textbooks, one of the best opportunities for students to increase their skill with technical or procedural text.

Slow Reading in Math: The Textbook

Close reading of math textbooks is undervalued. Close reading could give students regular opportunities to practice and hone their "technical reading" ability from texts that include procedures, directions, and instructional manuals. The world we live in will increasingly require the knack of making sense of such text.

In the last two chapters, we looked at the findings from Shanahan and Shanahan's two-year study on the use and value of textbooks. We've seen how they recommend slow, careful, reiterative reading in all of the content areas. The Shanahans found that of all content areas, mathematical text must be read most carefully of all. Every word and sentence is of great importance. Math procedures, explanations, and story problems must always be read slowly and repeatedly and never for mere "gist or general idea." The meaning in math text often pivots on the use of a single word; in many word problems, inattention to the distinction between "a" and "the" will result in misunderstanding. They note that the ideas and operations in a math text or story problem "require a precision of meaning and each word must be understood especially to the particular meaning" (2008, p. 49). Or, as Braselton and Decker (1994) write,

> Mathematics is the most difficult content area material to read because there are more concepts per word, per sentence, and per paragraph than in any other subject; the mixture of words, numerals, letters, symbols, and graphics requires the reader to shift from one type of vocabulary to another. (p. 276)

I am now looking at an elementary grade math problem that asks for interpretation of a Venn diagram. The diagram represents polling data. Only after reading the story problem twice, slowly, and then rereading some phrases several times did it become clear to me that the correct answer hinges on the use of the single word "might" (as opposed to "is"). The diagram reveals that a certain individual might (or might not) belong in both categories.

If I were a teacher, my students would need to hear all of my thought processes as I read such a problem to see where I read and reread, where I became puzzled, and how, as an adult, I read methodically to reach an understanding of the problem.

The average student simply isn't sensitive to language at this level of precision—and often doesn't realize that even adults engage in "slow reading" to acquire meaning. To ensure that students acquire these important reading habits, we must model such reading on a frequent basis. Here's how slow reading looks in an effective math lesson.

The First "R" in Math: Reading

Arthur Hyde is a professor of mathematics education. He is convinced that dramatic improvement will occur in all schools only when we are willing to embrace an "essential change": We must put whole-class, word-by-word, sentence-by-sentence "reading comprehension" at the center of math instruction (Hyde, 2007, p. 44). Math educators must redouble their efforts to "infuse language and thought into mathematics" (p. 46).

Let's look at his simple example of how he and his K–8 teaching partners have achieved dramatic success on open-ended, extended-response, and word problems. Their work is a model of the power of effective whole-class instruction—with ample opportunities for guided practice, checks for understanding, and ongoing adjustment to instruction and the goal of ensuring that all students learn.

The 2nd grade lesson begins like any good reading lesson, with the teacher providing essential background for the context of the problem and a review of potentially unfamiliar words that might impede understanding of the text (in this lesson, the word "freight"). In the next step, the teacher posts the word problem on the board or overhead projector. The teacher then guides students through a carefully scaffolded, whole-class, *sentence-by-sentence analysis* of the problem. For each sentence, students write their thoughts and answers as the teacher guides and advises them in their work. This is precisely the kind of "interplay of numbers and words" that makes math meaningful (Steen, 2007, p. 10). It is not unlike the line-by-line treatment we devote to a poem or to the word-by-word analysis that Rafe Esquith has his 5th grade students do for challenging documents like the Declaration of Independence.

Using such close slow-reading methods, Hyde and his K–8 teachers have been able to get 2nd grade students to succeed on complex, multistep math problems that most would deem too challenging for 2nd graders. But as a result of such "adapted reading comprehension strategies," performance in math has "improved dramatically" (Hyde, 2007, p. 45).

As we saw in Chapter 3, such teacher-directed, whole-class approaches have been shown to work with students in Singapore—

"for students who perform on, above or below grade level" (Hoven & Garelick, 2007, p. 30).

For students to understand math, they need direct, intensive reading instruction. Reading—the first "R"—is critical. But so is the second "R": writing. We must be ever mindful that writing is not only a form of communication, it is perhaps the best tool we know for problem solving. That makes writing an essential tool for teaching math effectively.

The Second "R" in Math: Writing

It is unfortunate that so many leave their teacher preparation programs without a deep, abiding knowledge that writing is perhaps the most powerful form of thinking, clarifying, and problem solving in any subject. In the late Ted Sizer's words, "Writing is the litmus paper of thought . . . the very center of schooling" (in Schmoker, 2006, p. 61).

The very act of writing allows us to see conceptual relationships, to acquire insights, and to unravel the logic of what was previously murky or confusing. We know that students can learn to "plug and chug" to get right answers on multiple-choice math tests (and this is not all bad). But we also know that this doesn't give them a sense of the underlying principles of the operations they learn in this way. When students are asked to explain or evaluate a solution or algorithm in writing, they come to a clearer, deeper understanding of a formula's meaning and application.

The effects of writing on learning and problem solving can be dramatic. In one middle school, 186 students were given multiple opportunities to explain and problem solve—in writing—as they learned math concepts. As a result, the percentage of students who met or exceeded performance standards on the state rubric rose from 4 to 75 percent in math knowledge, 19 to 68 percent in strategic knowledge, and 8 to 68 percent on math explanations (Zollman,

2009). As the author writes, "good teaching in reading and writing is good teaching in math" (p. 11).

Writing simultaneously teaches us to express ourselves precisely. As Steen discovered, employers will always "seek graduates who can interpret data . . . and can communicate effectively about quantitative topics." Therefore,

> K–12 students need extensive practice *expressing verbally* the quantitative meanings of both problems and solutions. They need to be able to *write fluently in complete sentences and coherent paragraphs*; to explain the meaning of data, tables, graphs and formulas . . . synthesize information, make sound assumptions, capitalize on ambiguity and *explain their reasoning.* (Steen, 2007, p. 12, my emphasis)

But K–12 students rarely get such "extensive practice." As a result, even college students in the natural and social sciences have a hard time "expressing in precise English the meaning of data presented in tables and graphs" (Steen, 2007, p. 11). From the earliest grades, students need far more opportunities—in math and in all the disciplines—to write explanations and interpretations of calculations or quantitative arguments or a graph on global warming, health care, or teen smoking.

Writing may be among the most vital but missing ingredients in current math education. As math expert Marilyn Burns (2004) writes, "I can no longer imagine teaching math without making writing an integral aspect of students' learning. . . . Writing in math class requires students to organize, clarify, and reflect on their ideas" (p. 30). There are plenty of exquisitely simple ways to write in math. All of them exercise students' critical and mathematical reasoning capacities and the ability to give verbal form to numbers and equations. Doug Reeves (2007) recommends one of my favorite strategies: for selected multiple-choice items, have students write explanations for why any one of the incorrect choices is wrong. A variation on this is recommended by Tim Kanold, textbook author and former math teacher and superintendent of Adlai Stevenson High School. At Stevenson, students can receive credit for incorrect answers on their tests if they will explain, in writing, why their answer was wrong and why the correct answer is right.

To deepen conceptual understanding, Marilyn Burns has students routinely write explanations and descriptions for any math concept they are taught. For example, 3rd graders are asked to write an explanation for concepts such as "equally likely," 4th graders are asked to write about how multiplication and division are similar and different, and 5th graders are asked, at certain junctures in a unit on fractions, to *write a short essay* on the topic of "What I Know About Fractions So Far" (2004, p. 32, my emphasis).

Burns provides another simple, all-purpose writing strategy: Give students regular opportunities to explain why one answer or approach to a math problem is superior to another. She suggests a simple prompt with limitless applications at any level (2004, p. 33):

- I think that the answer is _____.
- I think that because _____.
- I figured this out by _____.

Simple enough? The benefits of such regular writing exercises would be immeasurable for mathematical and logical thinking (in any sphere). Perhaps they, too, should become one of the routine components of good math lessons.

There is also real value in occasional but more elaborate writing assignments in math. Some schools have built such formal written assignments or graduation projects into their math curriculum. I think this would be a valuable option for us to consider for the end of elementary, middle, and high school. For example, at a high school in Colorado, one of the graduation requirements was that students had to demonstrate, in writing, that they understood and could apply their knowledge of 17 essential math concepts. For each standard, they had to "demonstrate appropriate written communication of problem solving" for skills like

- Problems involving percents, ratios and proportions, simple and compound interest, maps and scale drawings;
- Interpretations of bar, line, and circle graphs; and
- Interpretations and analyses of statistical data (Littleton Public Schools, 1993).

At Central Park East in Harlem, New York, students must complete several written projects to graduate. The one for math requires students to:

Demonstrate higher order thinking ability by developing a project using mathematics for political, civic, or consumer purposes (e.g., social science statistics or polling, architectural blueprints) and either scientific or "pure" mathematics. (Cushman, 1993)

As mentioned previously in this book, the schools in the New York Performance Standards Consortium (NYPSC) require students to complete a serious, extended written project in each discipline in order to graduate. One student's math essay was on "Finding the Parabolic Path of a Comet as It Moves Through the Solar System." NYPSC students are exceptionally satisfied with their schools, and the school's follow-up studies find that they are far more prepared for college than their peers (Schmoker, 2009).

I wish my daughters could have had such an education. Such projects would ensure that students learn, in Lynn Steen's words, to "write fluently . . . explain their reasoning [and] . . . communicate effectively about quantitative topics" (2007, p. 12). Such projects could round out an engaging, robust, and practical math education—one that contributes to success in all other subjects.

Math is indeed pervasive. With some very deliberate, sensible adjustments, it could be made more meaningful for all of us in every sphere and could equip students to understand and apply it to their careers, their work as citizens, and their everyday lives like never before. All it will require is a logical review of what we teach and why, combined with a commitment to ensuring that every math lesson is an *effective* lesson that derives from a manageable coherent curriculum.

• • •

Thank you for getting this far. I do hope you'll now read my brief conclusion, which underscores some critical points.

Conclusion:
This Time, Let's Do It

There is always a temptation (for me anyway) to add fresh material in the concluding chapter of a book. Not this time. I would merely like to say: We know what to do, so please, let's do it. If you'll allow just a little more repetition in what has been an admittedly repetitious book:

We know what a sound, coherent curriculum is. Let's build one for every course we teach, with common assessments, and then actually monitor to ensure that it's being taught.

We know—now more than ever—that structurally sound lessons will literally multiply the number of students who will be ready for college, careers, and citizenship.

We know that students desperately need to do lots of meaningful reading and writing, along the lines described in these chapters, and that this does not necessitate inordinate amounts of paper grading. Let's stop making excuses for not doing it.

We know that the implementation of all of the above relies on our commitment to *monitor that implementation* and encourage teachers *to work in teams* to help each other to refine and improve on their design and execution. If they do, each of the above will improve dramatically and inexorably. It's that simple.

In closing, let me say that I only wish that my two daughters could have enjoyed the kind of education described by the writers, thinkers, and real-life practitioners profiled in this book. But for a few exceptions, my children did not receive such an education, even though they were in high-scoring schools and always in the honors track. But maybe, just maybe, their sons and daughters will someday receive an intellectually rich education because we learned, at long last, to focus "on what is essential and [to] ignore the rest" (Collins, 2001a, p. 91).

This time, let's not just talk about it. Let's all of us actually do it. Right now.

References

Ainsworth, L. (2003a). *Power standards*. Englewood, CO: Advanced Learning Press.

Ainsworth, L. (2003b). *"Unwrapping" the standards: A simple process to make standards manageable*. Englewood, CO: Advanced Learning Press.

Alberts, B. (2006–2007, December–January). Why I became a scientist. *Educational Leadership, 64*(4), 18.

Allington, R. L. (2001). *What really matters for struggling readers*. New York: Addison Wesley Longman.

Ancess, J. (2008, May). Small alone is not enough. *Educational Leadership, 65*(8), 48–49.

Azzam, A. (2008, March). Engaged and on track. *Educational Leadership, 65*(6), 93–94.

Banner, J. (2009, July 15). Assessing the teaching of history. *Education Week, 28*(36), 24–25.

Barzun, J. (1991). *Begin here*. Chicago & London: University of Chicago Press.

Bauerlein, M. (2008, September 19). Online literacy is a lesser kind. *Chronicle of Higher Education*. Retrieved August 16, 2010, from http://chronicle.com/article/Online-Literacy-Is-a-Lesser/28307.

Berliner, D. (1984). The half-full glass: A review of research on teaching. In P. Hosford (Ed.), *Using what we know about teaching* (pp. 51–77). Alexandria, VA: ASCD.

Berliner, D., & Biddle, B. (1995). *The manufactured crisis: Myths, fraud, and the attack on America's public schools*. Cambridge, MA: Perseus Books.

Bloom, A. (1988). *The closing of the American mind*. New York: Simon & Schuster.

Bracey, G. (2004, December). Value-added assessment findings: Poor kids get poor teachers. *Phi Delta Kappan, 86*(4), 331–333.

Braselton, S., & Decker, B. C. (1994). Using graphic organizers to improve the reading of mathematics. *The Reading Teacher, 48*(3), 276–287.

Buckingham, M. (2005). *The one thing you need to know: About great managing, great leading, and sustained individual success.* New York: Free Press.

Burns, M. (2004, October). Writing in math. *Educational Leadership, 62*(2), 30–33.

Burns, M. (2007). Nine ways to catch kids up. *Educational Leadership, 65*(3), 16–21.

BusinessWeek. (2000, April 24). The pros and cons of globalization. Retrieved September 3, 2010, from http://www.businessweek.com/2000/00_17/b3678003.htm.

Bybee, R., & Van Scotter, P. (2006–2007, December–January). Reinventing the science curriculum. *Educational Leadership, 64*(4), 43–47.

Cavanagh, S. (2007, June 12). What kind of math matters? Diplomas count: A report by *Education Week*. *Education Week, 26*(40), 21–23.

Collins, J. (2001a). *Good to great.* New York: Harper Business.

Collins, J. (2001b, October). Good to great. *Fast Company, 51*(1), 90–104.

Collins, J. (2005). *Good to great and the social sectors.* Boulder, CO: Author.

Colvin, R., & Johnson, J. (2007, October 31). Know the game and cover the action. *Education Week, 27*(19), 36.

Conley, D. (2005). *College knowledge: What it really takes for students to succeed and what we can do to get them ready.* San Francisco: Jossey-Bass.

Conley, D. (2007, April). The challenge of college readiness. *Educational Leadership, 64*(7), 23–29.

Cookson, P. (2009, September). Teaching for the 21st century. *Educational Leadership, 67*(1), 8–14.

Cunningham, P., & Allington, R. L. (2007). *Classrooms that work: They can all read and write.* Boston: Pearson.

Cushman, K. (1993). How the national standards debate affects the essential school [Online article]. Retrieved August 16, 2010, from http://www.essentialschools.org/resources/95.

Cushman, K. (2007, April). Facing the culture shock of college. *Educational Leadership, 64*(7), 44–47.

De Vise, D. (2006, December 5). Local schools to study whether math – topics = better math education. *Washington Post,* A1.

DuFour, R. (2007, Spring). Clarity is the key to skillful leadership. *Journal of Staff Development, 28*(2), 69.

DuFour, R., DuFour, R., Eaker, R., & Many, T. (2006). *Learning by doing: A handbook for professional learning communities at work.* Bloomington, IN: Solution Tree.

Duke, N. (2010, February). R&D: The real-world reading and writing U.S. children need. *Phi Delta Kappan, 91*(5), 68–71.

Edmundson, M. (2004). *Why read?* New York: Bloomsbury.

Elmore, R. F. (2000, Winter). *Building a new structure for school leadership.* Washington, DC: The Albert Shanker Institute.

Englemann, S., Haddox, P., & Bruner, E. (1983). *Teach your child to read in 100 easy lessons.* New York: Simon & Schuster.

Esquith, R. (2003). *There are no shortcuts.* New York: Random House.

Esquith, R. (2007). *Teach like your hair's on fire.* New York: Penguin Books.

Ferrandino, V. L., & Tirozzi, G. (2004, May 5). Wanted: A comprehensive literacy agenda preK–12. *Education Week, 23*(24), 29.

Fisher, D., & Frey, N. (2007). *Checking for understanding.* Alexandria, VA: ASCD.

Fitzhugh, W. (2006, October 4). Bibliophobia. *Education Week.* Retrieved August 16, 2010, from http://www.edweek.org/ew/articles/2006/10/04/06fitzhugh.h26.html.

Ford, M. P., & Opitz, M. F. (2002, May). Using centers to engage children during guided reading time: Intensifying learning experiences away from the teacher. *The Reading Teacher, 55*(8), 710–717.

Friedman, T. L. (2005). *The world is flat: A brief history of the 21st century.* New York: Farrar, Straus and Giroux.

Friedman, T. L. (2008). *Hot, flat and crowded.* New York: Farrar, Straus and Giroux.

Fuhrman, S. H., Resnick, L., & Shepard, L. (2009, October 14). Standards aren't enough. *Education Week, 9*(7), 28.

Gallagher, K. (2009). *Readicide: How schools are killing reading and what you can do about it.* Portland, ME: Stenhouse Publishers.

Gamerman, E. (2008, February 29). What makes Finnish kids so smart? *The Wall Street Journal.* Retrieved August 16, 2010, from http://online.wsj.com/article/NA_WSJ_PUB:SB120425355065601997.html.

Gardner, H. (2009, February). Five minds for the future. *The School Administrator, 66*(2), 16–21.

Garnaut, J. (2007, May 21). Best teachers get top marks from study. *Sydney Morning Herald.* Retrieved August 16, 2010, from http://www.smh.com.au/news/national/best-teachers-get-top-marks-from-study/2007/05/20/1179601244341.html.

Garner, D. (2010, March 12). Inferior national standards: English language arts. *EducationNews.org.* Retrieved August 16, 2010, from http://www.educationnews.org/commentaries/71559.html.

Gatto, J. T. (2002). *Dumbing us down.* Gabriola Island, Canada: New Society Publishers.

Gewertz, C. (2010, May 19). How to move from standards to curricula? *Education Week, 29*(32), 1, 22.

Goldberg, M. (2001, May). An interview with Linda Darling-Hammond: Balanced optimism. *Phi Delta Kappan, 82*(9), 687–690.

Gomez, L. M., & Gomez, K. (2007, November). Reading for learning: Literacy supports for 21st century learning. *Phi Delta Kappan, 89*(3), 224–228.

Goodlad, J. I. (1984). *A place called school.* New York: McGraw Hill.

Graff, G. (2003). *Clueless in academe.* New Haven, CT, and London: Yale University Press.

Graff, G., & Birkenstein, C. (2007). *"They say, I say": The moves that matter in persuasive writing.* New York: W. W. Norton & Company.

Hammond, B. (2009, November 7). More Oregon students are getting math. *The Oregonian.* Retrieved August 16, 2010, from http://www.oregonlive.com/education/index.ssf/2009/11/more_oregon_students_are_getti.html.

Hapgood, S., & Palincsar, A. S. (2006). Where literacy and science intersect. *Educational Leadership, 64*(4), 56–61.

Harlem Village Academies. (n.d.). [Website]. Retrieved September 7, 2010, from http://www.harlemvillageacademies.com.

Harrop, F. (2010, February 14). Slobs and American civilization. *Projo.com.* Retrieved August 11, 2010, from http://www.projo.com/opinion/columnists/content/Cl_froma14_02-14-10_15h8fas_v10.3f8d0ce.html.

Haycock, K. (2003, May 20). Testimony of Kati Haycock, President, the Education Trust, before the U.S. House of Representatives committee on education and the workforce subcommittee on 21st century competitiveness. Retrieved August 16, 2010, from http://www.edtrust.org/dc/press-room/statement-testimony/testimony-of-kati-haycock-president-the-education-trust-before-the.

Haycock, K. (2005, June 8). Improving academic achievement and closing gaps between groups in the middle grades. Presentation given at CASE Middle Level Summit.

Henig, R. M. (2009, December 23). A hospital how-to guide that Mother would love. *The New York Times.* Retrieved August 16, 2010, from http://www.nytimes.com/2009/12/24/books/24book.html.

Hernandez, A., Kaplan, M. A., & Schwartz, R. (2006, October). For the sake of argument. *Educational Leadership, 64*(2), 48–52.

Hillocks, G. (1987, May). Synthesis of research on teaching writing. *Educational Leadership, 44*(8), 71–82.

Hirsch, E. D. (2008, April 23). An epoch-making report, but what about the early grades? *Education Week, 27*(34), 30–31, 40.

Hirsch, E. D. (2009). *The making of Americans*. New Haven, CT, and London: Yale University Press.

Hirsch, E. D. (2010, January 14). First, do no harm. *Education Week, 29*(17), 30–31, 40.

Hoven, J., & Garelick, B. (2007, November). Singapore math: Simple or complex? *Educational Leadership, 65*(3), 28–31.

Hyde, A. (2007, November). Mathematics and cognition. *Educational Leadership, 65*(3), 43–47.

Ivey, G., & Fisher, D. (2006, October). When thinking skills trump reading skills. *Educational Leadership, 64*(2), 16–21.

Jago, C. (2005). *Papers, papers, papers*. Portsmouth, NH: Heinemann.

Kenny, C. (2010, September/October). Best. Decade. Ever. *Foreign Policy*. Retrieved September 7, 2010, from http://www.foreignpolicy.com/articles/2010/08/16/best_decade_ever?

Kohn, A. (2010, January 14). Debunking the case for national standards. *Education Week, 29*(17), 28, 30.

Kristoff, N. (2009, December 30). Sparking a savings revolution. *The New York Times*. Retrieved August 11, 2010, from http://www.nytimes.com/2009/12/31/opinion/31kristof.html.

Kurtz, S. (2007, September 14). *Closing*, still open. *National Review*. Retrieved August 11, 2010, from http://article.nationalreview.com/327385/iclosingi-still-open/stanley-kurtz.

Landsberg, M. (2008a, March 11). In L.A. Singapore math has added value. *Los Angeles Times*, A2.

Landsberg, M. (2008b, June 21). Teacher instills a love of words, but the lesson is about life. *Los Angeles Times*. Retrieved August 16, 2010, from http://www.icefla.org/ourpages/auto/2008/10/6/1223312636225/Teacher%20Instills%20a%20Love%20of%20Words%20--%20The%20Los%20Angeles%20Times%20June%2020%202008.pdf.

Leinwand, S., & Ginsburg, A. L. (2007, November). Learning from Singapore math. *Educational Leadership, 65*(3), 32–36.

Littleton Public Schools. (1993). *Demonstration book: Directions 2000*. Littleton CO: Directions 2000 Foundation; Littleton Public Schools.

Loewen, J. (1995). *Lies my teacher told me*. New York: Touchstone.

Lunsford, A. A., & Ruszkiewicz, J. J. (2009). *Everything's an argument*. New York: Bedford St. Martin's.

Maranto, R., Ritter, G., & Levine, A. (2010, January 6). The future of ed. schools. *Education Week, 29*(16), 25, 36.

Marzano, R. J. (2003). *What works in schools: Translating research into action.* Alexandria, VA: ASCD.

Marzano, R. J. (2007). *The art and science of teaching.* Alexandria, VA: ASCD.

Marzano, R. (2009, October 9). Helping students process information. *Educational Leadership, 67*(2), 86–87.

Marzano, R., & Kendall, J. S. (1998). *Awash in a sea of standards.* Denver, CO: McREL.

Marzano, R. J., Pickering, D. J., & Pollock, J. E. (2001). *Classroom instruction that works.* Alexandria, VA: ASCD.

Mathews, J. (2010, February 22). Help pick non-fiction for schools. *The Washington Post.* Retrieved September 7, 2010, from http://voices.washingtonpost.com/class-struggle/2010/02/help_pick_non-fiction_for_scho.html.

Mazur, E. (1997). *Peer instruction: A user's manual.* Upper Saddle River, NJ: Prentice-Hall.

McConachie, S., Hall, M., Resnick, L., Ravi, A. K., Bill, V. L., Bintz, J., & Taylor, J. A. (2006, October). Task, text, and talk. *Educational Leadership, 64*(2), 8–14.

McKeown, M. G., Beck, I. L., & Blake, R. K. (2009, July/August/September). Rethinking reading comprehension instruction: A comparison of instruction for strategies and content approaches. *Reading Research Quarterly, 44*(3), 218–253.

Meier, D. (2010, April). Are national standards the right move? *Educational Leadership, 67*(7), 23.

Mortimore, P., & Sammons, P. (1987, September). New evidence on effective elementary schools. *Educational Leadership, 45*(1), 4–8.

National Commission on Writing. (2003, April). *The neglected "r": The need for a writing revolution.* New York: The College Board.

Ness, M. (2007, November). Reading comprehension strategies in secondary content-area classrooms. *Phi Delta Kappan, 89*(3), 229–231.

Odden, A. (2009, December 9). We know how to turn schools around—we just haven't done it. *Education Week, 29*(14), 22–23.

Odden, A., & Wallace, M. J. (2003, August 6). Leveraging teacher pay. *Education Week, 22*(43), 64.

Olson, L. (2008, May 10). Skills for work, college readiness are found comparable. *Education Week, 25*(36), 1, 19.

O'Rourke, P. J. (2005, March 16). Mass transit hysteria. *The Wall Street Journal,* A24.

Packer, A. (1997). Mathematical competencies that employers expect. In Lynn Steen (Ed.), *Why numbers count* (pp. 137–154). New York: The College Board.

Packer, A. (2007, November 7). Know what the real goals are. *Education Week.* Retrieved August 16, 2010, from http://www.edweek.org/ew/articles /2007/11/07/11packer.h27.html.

Perkins-Gough, D. (2006–2007, December–January). The status of the science lab. *Educational Leadership, 64*(4), 93–94.

Pfeffer, P., & Sutton, R. (2000). *The knowing-doing gap.* Boston: Harvard Business School Press.

Phillips, V., & Wong, C. (2010, February). Tying together the common core of standards, instruction, and assessments. *Phi Delta Kappan, 91*(5), 37–42.

Pianta, R., Belsky, J., Houts, R., & Morrison, F. (2007, March). Teaching: Opportunities to learn in America's elementary classrooms. *Science, 315*(5820), 1795–1796.

Podhoretz, N. (1967). *Making it.* New York: Harper Colophon.

Pollack, H. (1997). Solving problems in the real world. In Lynn Steen (Ed.), *Why numbers count* (pp. 91–105). New York: The College Board.

Popham, W. J. (2008). *Transformative assessment.* Alexandria, VA: ASCD.

Ravitch, D. (2010, January 14). We've always had national standards. *Education Week, 29*(17), 28, 30.

Reeves, D. B. (2003). *Accountability for learning.* Alexandria, VA: ASCD.

Reeves, D. B. (2004). *Accountability in action* (2nd ed.). Englewood, CO: Lead & Learn Press.

Reeves, D. B. (2007, January 4). Top five tips to use student writing to improve math achievement. *Center for Performance Assessment Update.*

Reeves, D. B. (2008). *Reframing teacher leadership to improve your school.* Alexandria, VA: ASCD.

Ripley, A. (2010, January/February). What makes a great teacher? *Atlantic Monthly.* Retrieved August 16, 2010, from http://www.theatlantic.com/ magazine/archive/2010/01/what-makes-a-great-teacher/7841/.

Rose, M. (1989). *Lives on the boundary.* New York: Viking Penguin.

Roseman, J. E., Linn, Y., & Koppal, M. (2008). Characterizing curriculum coherence. In Y. Kali, M. Linn, & J. E. Roseman (Eds.), *Designing coherent science education* (pp. 13–36). New York: Teachers College Press.

Rosenholtz, S. J. (1991). *Teacher's workplace: The social organization of schools.* New York: Teachers College Press.

Roth, K., & Garnier, H. (2006–2007, December–January). What science teaching looks like: An international perspective. *Educational Leadership, 64*(4), 16–23.

Rotherham, A. J. (2008, December 15). 21st-century skills are not a new education trend but could be a fad. *U.S. News and World Report.* Retrieved August 16, 2010, from http://politics.usnews.com/opinion/articles/2008/12/15/21st-century-skills-are-not-a-new-education-trend-but-could-be-a-fad.html.

Sanders, W. L., & Horn, S. P. (1994, October). The Tennessee value-added assessment system. *Journal of Personnel Evaluation Education, 8*(3), 299–311.

Schlechty, P. (1990). *Schools for the 21st century.* San Francisco: Jossey-Bass.

Schlechty, P. (1997). *Inventing better schools.* San Francisco: Jossey-Bass.

Schmidt, W. H. (2008, Spring). What's missing from math standards? Focus, rigor, and coherence. *American Educator, 32*(1), 22–24.

Schmoker, M. (2001). *The results fieldbook: Practical strategies from dramatically improved schools.* Alexandria, VA: ASCD.

Schmoker, M. (2006). *Results now: How we can achieve unprecedented improvements in teaching and learning.* Alexandria, VA: ASCD.

Schmoker, M. (2008–2009, December–January). Measuring what matters. *Educational Leadership, 66*(4), 70–74.

Schmoker, M. (2009, July 7). Do we really need a longer school year? *Education Week.* Retrieved August 16, 2010, from http://www.edweek.org/ew/articles/2009/07/07/36schmoker.h28.html.

Science Daily. (2008, July 18). Students who use "clickers" score better on physics tests. Retrieved September 7, 2010, from http://www.sciencedaily.com/releases/2008/07/080717092033.htm.

Shanahan, T., & Shanahan, C. (2008, Spring). Teaching disciplinary literacy to adolescents: Rethinking content-area literacy. *Harvard Educational Review, 78*(1), 40–59.

Silva, E. (2008, November 10). Measuring skills for the 21st century. *Education Sector.* Retrieved August 16, 2010, from http://www.educationsector.org/usr_doc/MeasuringSkills.pdf.

Silver, H. F., Strong, R. W., & Perini, M. J. (2007). *The strategic teacher: Selecting the right research-based strategy for every lesson.* Alexandria, VA: ASCD.

Singham, M. (2005). *The achievement gap in U.S. education: Canaries in the mine.* Lanham, MD: Rowman & Littlefield Education.

Smith, F. (2006). *Reading without nonsense.* New York: Teachers College Press.

St. Jarre, K. (2008, May). Reinventing social studies. *Phi Delta Kappan, 89*(9), 649–652.

Steen, L. A. (2007, November). How mathematics counts. *Educational Leadership, 65*(3), 8–15.

Stiggins, R. (1994). *Student-centered classroom assessment.* New York: Merrill.

Traub, J. (1998, October 26). Multiple intelligence disorder. *The New Republic, 4*(371), 20–23.

Trefil, J. (2008). *Why science?* New York: Teachers College Press.

Vassilaros, D. (2008, October 10). Columbus was a hero. *Pittsburgh Tribune-Review.* Retrieved August 11, 2010, from http://www.pittsburghlive.com/x/pittsburghtrib/opinion/columnists/vassilaros/s_592550.html.

Wagner, T. (2008, November 12). Teaching and testing the skills that matter most. *Education Week, 28*(12), 30.

Wenglinsky, H. (2004, September). Facts or critical thinking skills? What NAEP results say. *Educational Leadership, 62*(1), 32–35.

Wenglinsky, H., & Silverstein, S. C. (2006–2007, December–January). The science training teachers need. *Educational Leadership, 64*(4), 24–29.

Wheeler, G. F. (2006–2007, December–January). Strategies for science education reform. *Educational Leadership, 64*(4), 30–34.

Wiggins, G. (1998). *Educative assessment.* San Francisco: Jossey-Bass.

Wiliam, D. (2007). Content then process: Teacher learning communities in the service of formative assessment. In D. Reeves (Ed.), *Ahead of the curve: The power of assessment to transform teaching and learning* (pp. 182–204). Bloomington, IN: Solution Tree.

Willingham, D. (2008, December 1). Education for the 21st century: Balancing content knowledge with skills. *Encyclopedia Britannica Blog.* Retrieved August 16, 2010, from http://www.britannica.com/blogs/2008/12/schooling-for-the-21st-century-balancing-content-knowledge-with-skills/.

Willingham, D. (2009a, September 28). Reading is not a skill—and why this is a problem for the draft national standards. *Washington Post.* Retrieved August 16, 2010, from http://voices.washingtonpost.com/answer-sheet/daniel-willingham/willingham-reading-is-not-a-sk.html.

Willingham, D. (2009b). *Why don't students like school?* San Francisco: Jossey-Bass.

Wineburg, S. (2001). *Historical thinking and other unnatural acts.* Philadelphia, PA: Temple University Press.

Wineburg, S., & Martin, D. (2004, September). Reading and rewriting history. *Educational Leadership, 62*(1), 42–45.

Wolk, R. (2010, April). Education: The case for making it personal. *Educational Leadership, 67*(7), 16–21.

Zakaria, F. (2008). *The post-American world.* New York: W. W. Norton & Company.

Zinn, H. (2003). *A people's history of the United States.* New York: Harper Perennial Modern Classics.

Zinn, H. (Adapted by Stefoff, R.) (2007/2009). *A young people's history of the United States.* New York: Seven Stories Press.

Zmach, C. C., Sanders, J., Patrick, J. D., Dedeoglu, H., Charbonnet, S., Henkel, M., Fang, Z., Lamme, L. L., & Pringle, R. (2006–2007, December–January). Infusing reading into science learning. *Educational Leadership, 64*(4), 62–66.

Zollman, A. (2009, November). Students use graphic organizers to improve mathematical problem-solving communications. *Middle School Journal, 41*(2), 4–12.

Index

Related ASCD Resources: Improvements in Teaching and Learning

At the time of publication, the following resources were available; for the most up-to-date information about ASCD resources, go to www.ascd.org. ASCD stock numbers are noted in parentheses.

Professional Interest Communities

Visit the ASCD Web site (www.ascd.org) and click on "Community." Go to the section on "Professional Interest Communities" for information about professional educators who have formed groups around topics like "Literacy, Language, and Literature," "Quality Education," and "Restructuring Schools." Click on "Professional Interest Communities Directory" for current facilitators' contact information.

ASCD EDge Group

Exchange ideas and connect with other educators interested in improvements in teaching and learning on the social networking site ASCD EDge™ at http://ascdedge.ascd.org/.

Print Products

The Art and Science of Teaching: A Comprehensive Framework for Effective Instruction, by Robert J. Marzano (#107001)

Accountability for Learning: How Teachers and School Leaders Can Take Charge, by Douglas B. Reeves (#104004)

Results: The Key to Continuous School Improvement, 2nd edition, by Mike Schmoker (#199233)

The Results Fieldbook: Practical Strategies from Dramatically Improved Schools, by Mike Schmoker (#101001)

Videotapes

What Works in Schools: School Factors with Robert J. Marzano (Tape 1; #403048)

The Results Video Series (two tapes) with Mike Schmoker (#401261)

THE WHOLE CHILD The Whole Child Initiative helps schools and communities create learningenvironments that allow students to be healthy, safe, engaged, supported, and challenged. To learn more about other books and resources that relate to the whole child, visit www.wholechildeducation.org.

For more information, visit us on the World Wide Web (http://www.ascd.org), send an e-mail message to member@ascd.org, call the ASCD Service Center (1-800-933-ASCD or 703-578-9600, then press 2), send a fax to 703-575-5400, or write to Information Services, ASCD, 1703 N. Beauregard St., Alexandria, VA 22311-1714 USA.

About the Author

Mike Schmoker is a former school administrator, English teacher, and (admittedly mediocre) football coach. He has written four books and dozens of articles for educational journals, newspapers, and *Time* magazine.

His last ASCD book, *Results Now: How We Can Achieve Unprecedented Improvements in Teaching and Learning* (2006), was selected as a finalist for book of the year by the Association of Education Publishers. His previous ASCD best-seller *Results: The Key to Continuous School Improvement* (1996) is one of the most widely used books by school leaders in the United States.

Dr. Schmoker has given keynote talks at hundreds of state, national, and international events and has consulted for school districts and state and provincial education departments throughout the United States, Canada, and Australia.

You can contact the author at 1842 E. Carver Rd., Tempe, AZ 85284; by phone at 480-219-4673; and by e-mail at schmoker@futureone.com.